LOTUS ELAN

Other Titles in the Crowood AutoClassics Series

Jaguar E-type	Jonathan Wood
Lamborghini Countach	Peter Dron
MGB	Brian Laban
Porsche 911	David Vivian
Ferrari Dino	Anthony Curtis

LOTUS ELAN
The Complete Story

Mike Taylor

GUILD PUBLISHING
LONDON · NEW YORK · SYDNEY · TORONTO

This edition published 1990 by
Guild Publishing
by arrangement with
The Crowood Press Ltd

Acknowledgements

The majority of the photographs in this Crowood AutoClassic
come from the National Motor Museum's Beaulieu photographic
library. Additional photographs are supplied by the author, Ron
Hickman and Robin Read.

Typeset by Action Typesetting Limited, Gloucester
Printed in Great Britain by Butler & Tanner Ltd, Frome

Contents

Foreword

When I joined Lotus in 1969, my family was still living in Kenilworth and I have very fond memories of commuting between Warwickshire and Hethel in an original Elan — memories that were revived whilst reading Mike Taylor's excellent new book on the car.

Despite having to squeeze my 6ft 5in frame into its compact cockpit, I always found the Elan great fun and very exhilarating to drive, achieving some excitingly quick A to B times. Its enjoyment was all about perfectly balanced handling and brakes, light, accurate steering and a free-revving engine which was fun to use.

With the original Elan, the lesson of volume production was learnt the hard way at Lotus — and it has to be said that this experience left some scars. But like all such experiences, this left a lasting impression which accounts for the almost obsessive care and attention to detail with which we now build the new Lotus range.

Life at Lotus in the intervening years since my arrival has been, to say the least, extremely exciting. The financial crisis the company has had to endure and the untimely death of its founder would have caused the downfall of lesser manufacturers. However, there is an indomitable spirit imbued in all the staff at Hethel which gains strength in such adversities.

In global terms, Lotus is only a very small

manufacturer, but it takes immense pride — and a lot of technology and innovation — in producing cars which set new world standards. The original Elan epitomises that attitude; its styling, handling and performance often put bigger, more powerful and costly cars to shame.

If you want to know the full story behind the Elan, then read on — Mike Taylor's book tells all.

Mike Kimberley
February 1990

ELAN: ELEVEN YEARS OF EVOLUTION

1962   October: new Lotus Elan 1500 roadster launched. UK list price £1,499, tonneau cover and heater extra. £1,095 in kit form. Ford-based tohc engine producing 100bhp. Ford Classic gearbox and 3.9 final drive. Disc brakes all round. All independent suspension, rack-and-pinion steering. Steel backbone chassis with GRP bodywork.

1963   May: engine size increased to 1,558cc (note, no Elans were sold with smaller 1,500cc engines) with 'Elan 1600' badge on wing sides. Hard-top now available as an option.

1964   November: introduction of Series 2 identified by 'S2' badges. Larger front brake callipers fitted, with centre lock road wheels available as an option together with smaller, foot pedals. Full width wood veneer dashboard with lockable glove box and chrome bezelled instruments. Rear light cluster now single oval unit and quick release filler cap added.

1965   September: introduction of Series 3 fixed-head coupe. High ratio 3.55 final drive available. Boot lid extended to rear of car and battery positioned in boot. Windows electrically operated. November: optional extras now include close ratio gearbox.

1966   January: launch of Special Equipment model. Standard features include more powerful 115bhp engine, close ratio gearbox, servo assisted disc brakes, centre lock road wheels and repeater flashes on front wing sides. June: introduction of Series 3 version of convertible. Details as for fixed hard-top model except for inclusion of frames to side windows.

1967   June: Elan +2 launched. All-new fixed hard-top model with longer, wider body to give greater cabin space. Similar build principle to Elan but with 118bhp engine and through-flow ventilation.

1968   March: Series 4 version of coupe and convertible Elan introduced. Flared wheelarches to accommodate wide profile tyres. Elan +2 rear light cluster adopted and revised facia to include safety-type rocker switches. Perforated seat trim and power bulge to bonnet. October: introduction of Elan Plus 2S with specification as +2 but with improved interior. Fog lights fitted as standard and '+2' badge on boot lid. First Elan not to be offered in kit form. November: Weber carburettors replaced by Strombergs on all models except Plus 2S.

1969   August: Stromberg carburettors replaced by Webers on Series 4 fhc and convertible. December: Elan +2 discontinued, Plus 2S remains in production.

1971   February: Elan Sprint introduced with 126bhp engine, with stronger driveshafts, couplings and differential. Model identified by two-tone paintwork. Elan Plus 2S 130 introduced, powered by Elan Sprint engine. Colour schemes include silver roof as identification.

1972   October: Five-speed gearbox available as an optional extra on Plus 2S 130 with 'S/130/5' badge located on nearside rear quarter.

1973   August: Elan fhc and convertible discontinued.

Introduction

Lotus has always been a company which has fascinated me, together with its enigma of a boss: Colin Chapman, affectionately known as ACBC, standing for (as all Lotus enthusiasts know) Anthony Colin Bruce Chapman.

My interest in the Hethel-based firm was further heightened when, in late 1982, I visited the factory for a feature article I was writing for the journal *Alternative Cars*. My host for the day was the company's Engineering Director, Michael Kimberley, who showed me round the Chapman empire.

During my interview with Michael I questioned him closely about Colin's attitude towards running the company and whether he felt Chapman would ever retire. 'I think I can best answer that by telling you exactly what Colin himself would say to that question' replied Michael. 'He says that "Old man Ferrari is thirty years older than me and still going, so I reckon I have at least thirty years in the business".' Almost within days of these words ACBC was dead.

It is generally agreed that Chapman's interest in customers during the company's early days was limited, showing little patience in actually selling his products and little feeling for the Lotus clubs. However, as time went on his attitude changed considerably and he displayed a deep feeling for the Elans and +2s. (Witness Chapman's increased enthusiasm for the older models at the 1979, 1980 and 1981 Lotus Days at the factory.) Today, examples of these marques are maintained in a condition which is as good, if not better, than the day they left the production line – a tribute to Colin Chapman and his cars.

Finally, I would like to take this opportunity to thank all those who have helped in the research of this work including Albert Adams, Ian Adcock and his staff, Paul Bing, Bill Brown, Fred Bushell, Jeremy Coulter, Jerry Doe, Morris Dowton, Colin Fish, Clive Fleay, Janet Fleay, John Frayling, Ron Hickman, Michael Kimberley, Peter Kirwan-Taylor, Bernie Lawrence, Ivan Nollath, Tom Peters, Tony Rudd and Pat Thomas, and offer my grateful thanks to the many people who responded with letters and photographs after reading my plea for help in *Lotus World*.

1 Laying the Foundation

THE EARLY DAYS

Élan n. dash, vigour, style, flair, flourish, panache . . .

The Lotus Elan was more than accurately named, for the dictionary definition of the word could equally describe the qualities of the man who founded the company that made it.

The only son of Stanley and Mary Chapman, Anthony Colin Bruce Chapman was born on 19 May 1928 in Richmond, Surrey where his father owned The Orange Tree public house. The Chapmans later moved to the Railway Hotel in Tottenham Lane, Hornsey in North London and at the outbreak of the Second World War Colin was evacuated to Wisbech in Cambridgeshire. By 1944 Colin had returned to London to attend the Stationers' Company School and despite the upheaval of war, he nevertheless set his sights on university.

No matter what Mr Hitler had in mind for Britain, 1944 proved to be a significant year for Colin Chapman's personal future, for in March, at a local dance organised by his father, he met an attractive, dark-haired girl from Muswell Hill. Her name was Hazel Williams, a trainee secretary. Hazel has said that although both she and Colin were very shy, she was immediately attracted by the apparent confident way in which he approached everyday things. Suffice it to say that the trainee secretary must have found the aspiring young engineer sufficiently personable to meet him the following day when they cycled to Friern Barnet to play golf.

In 1945, Colin Chapman began a three-year course in engineering at London University and it was not long before he uprated his means of transport by buying a 350cc Panther motor bike. Like most anxious mothers though, Mrs Williams was not too happy about her daughter riding pillion. She need not have worried because Hazel's motor-cycling days were soon brought to an abrupt end when Colin had an argument with a taxi while riding solo! However, Christmas was looming and Chapman's parents presented their son with a smart, maroon 1937 Morris 8 Tourer.

Despite the restrictions imposed by fuel rationing, demand for cars in the immediate post-war period was high. As a result, the second-hand car market began to flourish and the cheap 'banger' became particularly sought after. Not surprisingly, Colin began wheeling and dealing in this area but while Hazel's father could sometimes be persuaded to help him with his finances, Chapman senior was less than happy with these activities.

With his characteristic enthusiasm and single-mindedness, the banger business occupied much of Colin's spare time. But despite all this effort, Colin invariably was short of cash. Saturday evenings, however, were always kept aside for attending a local dance or the occasional trip to the cinema where, apparently, he would creep in through a side-door in order to side-step the tricky business of having to purchase a ticket!

Colin progressed well at university. A few days spent reading up before an exam seemed all that he needed to acquire the necessary information with which to pass.

In October 1947 basic petrol rationing was abolished and demand for the kind of cars Colin dealt in fell dramatically. After calculating what profit he had made over the year against the money he was able to realise from he sale of his 'stock' he emerged with exactly nothing! However, the experience had been valuable, if nothing else.

CHAPMAN MAKES HIS MARK

At this point, Colin decided to try his hand at motor sport and bought a 1930 Austin Seven fabric-bodied saloon. Working in a lock-up garage behind Hazel's home, the car was stripped down and converted into a 'special'. The chassis was modified by welding a fourth side to the 'U' section chassis, the front beam axle was split in the centre, the engine was rebuilt and the rear axle inverted to overcome axle steer under heavy cornering. Finally, a pretty but functional alloy body was added with a distinctive grille. The effectiveness of this car (retrospectively known as the Mark I Lotus) was shown in 1948 when the car was entered in two trials, both of which gained Chapman class awards.

In 1948 Colin graduated from university with a degree in civil engineering. His particular speciality was structural engineering, a subject which without doubt would help enormously when he later began designing cars. First, however, there was a new challenge waiting on the horizon – flying. He had already completed some thirty-five hours of flying with the University Air Squadron and gained his private pilot's licence. What better way to go flying than at someone else's expense? So Colin took up a short-term commission with the RAF.

Soon after joining the RAF, Colin began building his second car. He created so much interest among the eleven other people on the same course that it was not long before five other enthusiasts were building Austin Seven 'specials', too. Anxious to get the most they could from their young officers, the RAF kept Chapman pretty busy during 1949 and precious little time was spent on building cars (and probably even less on courting the delightful Hazel, whose main contribution to the relationship seemed to be as project assistant). Even at this stage in his life Chapman could be hailed as ingenious. One example is the way he meshed a 42-tooth crown wheel with a 9-tooth pinion in the differential, filling the casing with Bluebell (a household cleaner) as a mild abrasive to bed-in the teeth. After fifty miles the liquid was changed for final drive fluid and Colin had produced the non-standard 4.55:1 ratio he wanted by utilising two off-the-shelf components!

With its boxed chassis and split front axle, the Mark II was similar in shape to the first car with separate front cycle wings and basic protection from the elements. Funds were always desperately short during this period (when were they not?) so a very worn Ford side-valve engine was bought for £5. From the beginning, though, it was clear that the old wheezy Ford 8 engine was too worn to give the car the performance it deserved. But, as luck would have it, a sharp deal between a Midlands-based firm who dealt in Ford parts, a local fire-damaged car which was complete with an almost-new engine and a breakers yard culminated in Colin acquiring the power unit he needed – and making a £5 profit into the bargain.

In September 1949 Colin gained his wings and was offered the opportunity to sign on for a further five years with a permanent commission. The idea did not appeal and Chapman was 'promoted' to the rank of Mister. A business contact of Stanley Chapman who owned Cousins, a construction firm, offered

Colin a job which he took. Unfortunately, the work schedule demanded that Colin be at his desk by 7 a.m., which was hardly compatible with the late hours he kept working on his car. Much to the chagrin of Chapman senior, Colin left to join British Aluminium, the move allowing him more gentlemanly hours. Not surprisingly, the relationship between father and son became a little strained for a while as a result.

For the 1950 season, Colin left the specification for his car almost standard, save for a higher compression ratio and stronger valve springs. The first six months proved very busy as Colin and Hazel prepared for and entered nineteen events between February and July – and won many 'pots' along the way. Colin soon began to realise that while all this activity was fun, it involved a large degree of luck and had nothing whatsoever to do with engineering talent. So the Mark II was sold (it was later seen in the Bolting Brothers' film *Brothers in Law*) along with the Mark I in an effort to generate the much-needed cash for Colin Chapman's next project.

THE CAR TO BEAT

The foundation for the Mark III was another Austin Seven, purchased for just £15. Again, the 'A' frame was boxed in but, to further aid rigidity, a triangular-shaped structure assembled from tubular steel was added above the engine and held in place by three bolts. The front suspension utilised a split Ford axle with transverse springs while at the rear was an Austin Seven final drive. Colin paid considerable attention to weight engineering and each element was meticulously weighed. When finished, the entire car tipped the scales at 815lb (369.7 kg).

Equal attention was paid to the construction of the engine and in particular the very basic Austin Seven induction system. Colin designed a special four-tube inlet manifold, welding a wall along the inside of each siamesed inlet tract, thereby splitting it in two. A down-draught twin choke carburettor from a Ford V8 engine completed the modification. It seems that no one had given much thought to this problem, competitors content to acknowledge the rules of the 750 Motor Club (MC). To say that Chapman's remedy was a success is an understatement: the rules were subsequently changed to prevent a similar modification being fitted in the future.

The 1951 season proved a great success and a look back over the list of entries indicated how well the car had performed against its rivals. Not only that, but now other competitors were asking Colin to build them replicas of the Mark III. Almost overnight, Colin Chapman was the man to beat and the designer and builder of the most competitive car.

At this point, extra space was needed to expand the work of designing and building cars and on 1 January 1952, Lotus Engineering Company was set up in the rear of Chapman's father's stables in Tottenham Lane, Hornsey. Colin retained his job with British Aluminium, working at that during the day and on the cars at night. It was not long before a board with the company name (and now famous ACBC logo) was to be seen outside the workshop. Inside, feverish activities extended well into the night and the strange cacophony of sounds attracted a whole host of enthusiasts, many of whom simply picked up some tools and joined in the fun.

Progress on the Mark IV car was not as quick as had been hoped but finally it was ready for delivery. Like its predecessors it was based on an Austin Seven chassis with suspension similar to that used on the Mark III. Power was provided by a Ford engine driving a three-speed Ford gearbox. The car proved very successful in club events throughout 1953 and well into 1954. The Mark V was to have been a 100mph (160.9kph) trials car with similar engineering to that of the Mark III but the time which had to be spent dealing with customers got in the way of proceeding with this project.

Experience with these early designs confirmed Chapman's theories on rigid chassis frame structures combined with soft suspension set-ups. With the next car, Colin started with a clean sheet of paper. No longer limited by the features integral with the Austin Seven chassis, he produced a multi-tubular structure, each section stress-calculated so that there was no superfluous weight. Again, experience with the previous cars showed that Ford parts were cheap, reliable and easy to buy so the front and rear axles, brakes, gearbox and wheels all came from the Dagenham parts bin. The result was the first in a long line of legendary Chapman sports racers: the Mark VI.

The very first car was built specifically for trials and was therefore set very high from the ground. The front suspension utilised a swing axle arrangement (as in Colin's earlier designs), although the significant difference was the use of coil spring/damper units in place of the transverse leaf springs at the front. The rear axle was a Ford unit with a fore-shortened prop shaft and torque tube so that it would fit the car's dimensions. The axle was mounted on coil spring/damper units located by a Panhard rod. The simple alloy bodywork was produced by a local specialist coachbuilder, Williams & Pritchard. The engineering was such that the total weight of the chassis/body unit was just 90lb (40.8kg).

Colin's idea was that the Mark VI would be sold as a kit of parts, the purchaser then adding more components, some of which would be modified by Lotus. The point of the scheme was that it neatly side-stepped the regulations concerning paying purchase tax (the fore-runner of VAT) which was levied on new cars but not new parts.

Good publicity from the car's perform-

A Lotus VI at Brands Hatch in June 1957. In the early days it was this model of Lotus which helped the company to become recognised as sports and racing car manufacturers.

ances, combined with advertising which Colin had placed in motoring journals, had their effect and orders began coming in. Cash flow was down to a trickle though, since it took time to build the cars before they could be sold and the prototype had been written off in a crash.

LOTUS IS ESTABLISHED

By Christmas 1952, the insurance money from the crashed Mark VI had arrived and things began to look brighter once more. In February 1953 Colin borrowed the now legendary £25 from Hazel to set up the business as a limited company and customers soon found that the stationery they received now read 'Lotus Engineering Co. Ltd.' on rather smart yellow paper with green printing with the names of the directors: ACB Chapman BSc (Eng) and HP Williams.

Although the company was now firmly established, finances were at a low ebb – far too low to actually pay any wages. It was through Adam Currie (owner of an early Lotus) that Colin met two engineer/draughtsmen from the De Havilland Aircraft Company – Peter Ross and 'Mac' McIntosh – who spent their evenings helping Colin with drawings and calculating stress factors. Like so many 'special' builders, Colin was finding that the transition from one-off 'specials' to production-line assembly was something more than just repeating the same job over again. A casual comment to another young engineer on the De Havilland payroll brought Colin into contact with someone who was to have a fundamental effect on the course of Lotus during those hectic early days, Mike Costin.

'At the time I met Colin I was working on the first air-conditioning systems for aircraft' said Mike, 'and I was introduced as a likely person who could help with the development

of his cars. I liked his engineering approach. Colin had orders for these cars and I became involved with the hacking and slashing which went into the Lotus kits. In fact, having built the first Mark VI we had to knock a wall of the workshop down to get the car out because at the time the door wasn't wide enough.'

The Mark VI production line was based upon sub-contracting assembly work to available enthusiasts. Dave Kelsey, who set up The Progress Chassis Company with John Teychenne (a school-friend of Colin Chapman), was commissioned to build the Mark VI chassis. The finished units were then delivered to the Lotus factory at Hornsey where Len Pritchard and his partner Charlie Williams (by now Williams & Pritchard had taken over a corner of the Hornsey workshop) would fit the body panels. Come knocking-off time and the evening shift would appear in the shape of Colin Chapman and Mike Costin who would assemble the car so that all the customer had to do was install the engine and running gear, and trim the interior. Meanwhile, Hazel would be catching up with the paperwork and supplying endless cups of tea.

Despite the cramped conditions of the little factory, the demand for the Mark VI over the next two years was such that Lotus produced around 100 cars. The majority of these were fitted with 1,172cc Ford side-valve units which made the Mark VI an ideal car to enter in the 750 MC events. As the 1953 season progressed, Chapman and Costin found time to build a works Mark VI to take racing. Colin was anxious to devise a way of tuning the engine to make it the fastest of its kind. The regulations stipulated that the camshaft should remain standard but there was nothing to stop the timing from being modified. (The club officials clearly had not counted on Chapman's ingenuity!) To circumvent the rules, Mike Costin produced a set of hand-made camshaft followers which featured concave faces and by doing so completely altered the rate at which the valves opened and closed.

'From the beginning, Colin's organisation was second-to-none' said Mike Costin. 'The specification for the Mark VI was a loose-leaf notebook with each page showing a particular component and how it had to be modified to make it into a Lotus part. Colin was the man of all men for neatness. He was brilliant and I was well aware of the fact.'

MAKING THE VIII

For the 1954 season, Chapman set himself the task of producing a car which would quite simply be the lightest, fastest and most stable car in its class. He sketched out some ideas for a full-width body, a shape not unlike the famous Bristol-engined car built by John Tojeiro. Costin was not impressed and brought in his brother Frank, an aerodynamicist with De Havilland's, to work on the Mark VIII project. Until then Frank's work had been centred around shapes which flew. Now he was being asked to produce a shape which would travel fast – Colin had estimated an all-up weight of 10cwt (508kg) with a power unit producing 85bhp and capable of 125mph (201.2kph) – but which stayed on the ground. Meanwhile, Colin and his team were busy designing and building the chassis. The structure was a fully triangulated set-up and a considerable amount of stress engineering was done to create the lightest, strongest form possible.

Frank visited Chapman at his Hornsey hideaway, took one look at the spidery chassis framework and commented that it *would* be good if it did not have all that extra weight. Costin, of course, was judging it by aircraft standards. From then on the two experts got on well. Chapman is reputed to have said that he did not want Frank to be brilliant for a week, he just wanted half an

hour of sheer genius. In Frank Costin he got more than his thirty minutes' worth. Costin produced a beautifully streamlined shape with a low, gradually sloping centre section nose and graceful front wing sections, the wing line being carried to large rear fins.

The front suspension utilised the Mark VI-type split front axle with coil spring/damper units, while at the rear was a de Dion axle with in-board brakes. Under the bonnet was an 1,250cc MG engine bored out to 1,498cc and fitted with a Laystall-Lucas alloy cylinder head with twin 1.75in (4.45 cm) SU carburettors. At the 1954 Grand Prix held at Silverstone in July, Colin won convincingly, beating the works Porsche 550 of Hans Herrmann.

Inevitably, demand for the Mark VIII increased and in order to make production easier, it was decided to utilise a modified version of the Mark VI chassis with additional struts to take the full-width bodyshell. However, Colin and Mike, in the works car, still managed to maintain an almost impossible schedule of race entries, all the more rigorous now since some events were abroad – and still be back in their respective offices on time on Monday mornings!

It was around this time that another man who would subsequently have a dramatic effect on Lotus came on the scene: Fred Bushell.

'At the time I was working for accountants Peat, Marwick, Mitchell & Co.' recalled Fred. 'Our paths crossed quite by chance when, one evening, I decided to walk home from the office and stopped off at a public convenience in Hornsey. Colin was using the facilities, dressed in his boiler suit and cloth cap. We struck up a conversation and I asked him what he was doing working so late. In reply he invited me to come and see and I found myself in this small workshop crammed full of sports cars. It was a hive of activity, almost like a private club.'

During the conversation Colin asked Fred

what his occupation was and on learning that he was an accountant asked if he would look at the books. Fred agreed to take on the work on a spare-time basis. Like everyone else, Fred fell under the Chapman charm, allowing himself to be infused by enthusiasm.

'It took about twelve months before we got to the point where we had customers coming through the door' said Fred, 'although those first dealings were simply a nightmare. There were arguments over the price and exactly what the customer got in his kit. It almost came to fisticuffs on more than one occasion. I thought, "This is ridiculous" so I said I would handle the next sale. I organised the invoice and called the customer, telling him when the car would be ready. On the day in question, Colin went off leaving me to complete the deal. When he returned he was amazed to find there had been very few problems and I'd got the money. Colin was a great one for delegating and suddenly I was the idiot who was dealing with these awful people called customers. I'd got myself a Saturday morning job.'

Next, Fred applied himself to the none-too-easy task of unravelling the customs and excise laws on the sale of component cars. He succeeded in reaching an agreement with the customs and excise officials over the composition of the Lotus kits that was acceptable to the department. As long as Lotus customers built the kits themselves, they would not be liable to any payment of tax, either then or in the future.

'I often worked twenty-four hours a day,' recalled Mike Costin. 'I'd go into De Havilland's every day loaded with bits for Lotus which needed plating or welding or whatever. During the race season, between March and September, I probably only slept about three or four times on a Friday night before a race. We did such stupid things, we even took Benzadrine tablets to stay awake.'

On 16 October 1954 Colin and Hazel were married in Northaw Church near Cuffley. Everyone from Lotus went along to wish them well. The old single-deck bus which was usually used as the team's race transporter was pressed into service for ferrying the guests to the little church and then on to the reception. Later, the happy couple left for a honeymoon in Majorca, although it seemed that even they could not escape from motor racing, for driver Reg Bicknell was staying at the same hotel.

By the end of the year, the combination of a full order book for 1955, an enthusiastic, conscientious and talented workforce, and the fact that Fred Bushell had taken control of financial matters convinced Colin that he should leave the cosy enclaves of British Aluminium and work full-time for Lotus. Mike Costin, too, felt that the little car company had now become sufficiently stable to enable him to resign from De Havilland's. The two men started their new full-time careers on 1 January 1955.

MARK IX AND X DEVELOPMENT

While demand for the Mark VIII remained strong, it was clear that some people warted to fit smaller 1,100cc engines, while other customers were thinking along the lines of more powerful 2-litre units such as the Bristol. To cater for those who wished to fit smaller engines, the Mark IX was launched. Shorter, with stubbier rear fins, the two works cars made their début in March 1955 and were specially designed to take the small Coventry–Climax engine. The Lotus Mark X utilised the same chassis frame as the Mark IX but, as it was being fitted with a heavier, more powerful engine, weight distribution was a prime consideration and the fuel tank and battery were relocated behind the rear axle. The rear suspension featured a de Dion arrangement and to handle the power, disc brakes were fitted all round. Only three Mark Xs were built during 1955. (Screen idol James Dean ordered one, but tragically was killed before taking delivery and another Mark X appeared in the feature film *Checkpoint.*)

1955 was significant in the evolution of Lotus because it was the first year Lotus took part in the Le Mans 24-Hours. A Mark IX, powered by a Coventry–Climax engine with disc brakes all round was entered in this prestigious race with Colin sharing the driving with race ace Ron Flockhart. However, in addition to being dogged by drivetrain problems, Colin spun off and was finally disqualified when he rejoined the race 'having failed to wait for the marshalls'.

As the number of orders increased, the major problem was the availability of space. Fred Bushell and Stan Chapman came to the rescue by buying a piece of land opposite the Tottenham Lane factory which they then loaned to Lotus. A large workshop and stores building was built on it and these facilities eased the problem considerably.

'I was with Lotus for ten years,' continued Mike Costin, 'and during that time it grew out of all proportion. We could and should have spent an awful lot more on equipment and resources than we did. It would have made the work a great deal easier.'

In 1955 the Lotus Engineering Company Limited was accepted into the ranks of the Society of Motor Manufacturers and Traders (SMMT) which made Chapman's enterprising little outfit eligible for exhibiting their products at the London Motor Show. Located in pole position (!) almost, on the ground floor amid the world's car makers, there was Lotus with a Mark IX, minus its body panels. Interest was considerable. No longer were Lotus just a name on the lips of the race fans, now the name of Lotus was being mentioned by the casual observer.

A running chassis of the Lotus Eleven at the 1955 Earls Court Show where it was enthusiastically received.

Without doubt, the Lotus Eleven was the sleekest yet. The basis was the now familiar triangulated chassis frame but the transmission tunnel was now a stressed alloy panel. The front suspension still retained the split axle system with coil spring/dampers and steering was by rack and pinion. The customer had the choice of three versions from which to choose: Sports, Club or Le Mans, which came with different engine, suspension and braking set-ups according to what the car was to be used for.

In 1957 the Lotus team was joined by the talented Keith Duckworth.

'Keith came to Lotus as a new boy but straight away I could see that he was brilliant,' recalled Mike Costin. 'I could see immediately that his approach was right and that whatever he was involved in had to work. However, Keith would argue with anybody and often there were disagreements between Keith and Colin. Often, I was the man keeping them apart.'

*Colin Chapman in the elegantly sleek Eleven sports racer which
was available in three different versions to suit every
pocket!*

*Another Eleven, this time at Brands Hatch in 1961, this car
could be fitted with a variety of engines from 1,100cc
Coventry–Climax to a 1,500cc Maserati unit.*

Many improvements to detail were made to the Eleven and these included the adoption of the double-wishbone suspension from the Lotus Twelve. The modified car became known as the Eleven Series 2 and made its début in 1957.

At Tottenham Lane, builders had been busy erecting more accommodation – an office block with a showroom, office space and draughtsmen's area above, together with a new office for Colin Chapman. A smart, illuminated sign proclaimed the name 'Lotus' above the showroom windows.

Enquiries for the little Mark VI continued to indicate that demand was, indeed, still there. A basic specification was drawn up and the Lotus Seven made its début at the 1957 Show. The foundation for the car was a spaceframe chassis similar to that used on the Eleven. The front suspension utilised double wishbones while the rear was a live axle with coil spring/damper units located by twin parallel trailing arms. Under the bonnet was the familiar 1,172cc Ford side-valve engine driving a three-speed gearbox. Lotus announced, perhaps a little boldly, that there were to be no special versions. The Seven was to be simply a Seven. However, the Seven was somewhat overshadowed by an all-new Lotus model which had taken its place on the company's stand at the 1957 Show. Indeed, the Mark Fourteen or Lotus Elite was the star of the show. Who can say what day-dreams Colin had allowed himself while he was tucked away working on his first car in the small lock-up garage behind Hazel's home?

SHAPING THE ELITE

There had been words of wisdom from Fred Bushell who urged Chapman to market a car which was not susceptible to the feast-and-

The Lotus Seven replaced the VI as the budget sports/racer and was produced between 1957 and 1960. The design was subsequently sold to Caterham Cars who continue to sell the car in a modified form as the Caterham Seven.

famine profile of the racing world and so would provide a stable financial income for the company. In developing the Elite, Chapman realised all these factors and more. The conversation which is said to have sparked off the Elite project took place in late 1955 between Colin Chapman and Peter Kirwan-Taylor, an accountant and regular visitor to Tottenham Lane who had already completed a Mark VI while still a student. It featured a special body designed by Kirwan-Taylor and built by Williams & Pritchard. Kirwan-Taylor put forward the idea of using a chassis fitted with a coupe body. However, for reasons of weight distribution, Chapman did not think that using the Eleven as the basis was right and felt that any closed coupe design should start from a clean sheet of paper. Kirwan-Taylor, already a gifted draughtsman with a feel for line and shape, began collecting his thoughts.

Without doubt, the two major factors which were to have an overwhelming effect on the final purity of shape for the Elite were the 'clean sheet of paper' approach and the decision to use a Coventry–Climax engine which would be angled heavily to the near-

Peter Kirwan-Taylor

Peter Kirwan-Taylor was born in 1930 and with the outbreak of World War II was evacuated to North America where he stayed for two years. His step-father was involved with Lagonda and through visits to see how WO Bently was progressing with designs for a new Lagonda, Peter became interested in automotive styling. Also, as a result of his step-father's association with Westland, Peter met and was greatly influenced by Teddy Petter, designer of the Westland Lysander, Whirlwind and Canberra bomber.

After leaving school, Kirwan-Taylor joined the Army (which included a spell with the SAS) for three years before going up to Trinity College, Cambridge to read economics. He then joined Peat, Marwick, Mitchell & Company where he was articled.

Meanwhile, Peter's interest in cars had led him to buy a Lotus Mark 6 (for which he designed a body himself) and this started his friendship with Colin Chapman. Then came a Swallow Doretti onto which he fabricated a new rear end complete with fixed hard-top.

The chance to style the Elite came from his suggestion to Chapman that he should design a coupe body for the latest Lotus Eleven. In reply, Chapman suggested that the project should be all-new and Peter submitted his new design concepts. After the first clay model was agreed little was done by way of modifications, the first Elite being sold to band leader Chris Barber. Kirwan-Taylor retained his ties with Lotus as one of the original directors of Lotus Cars until 1984 when the company was sold to Chrysler.

Peter Kirwan-Taylor, financial advisor to Colin Chapman and designer of the first Lotus Elite.

Before becoming involved with the shape for the Elite, Peter Kirwan-Taylor designed this sports car which was based on a Lotus VI chassis seen here at Brands Hatch in 1957.

side, thereby reducing its overall height in the car. This, in turn, allowed the scuttle height, bonnet line and wing proportions to be almost ideal, giving the Elite the classic shape fans rave over. Frank Costin's contribution was to adjust the shape around the front of the bonnet above the quarter lights and to give the car its cut-off Kamm-type tail. The result was a car with an impressive 0.29 coefficient of drag. Yet, for all that, it seems there was concern within the group that the drawings showed a simple, uncomplicated car which was far from exciting. How would the public react? This was 1956, remember, and mass-market models were heavily reliant upon overstatements of design with fins and an abundance of chrome to create appeal. The Elite followed no such trend.

Mechanically, the car would utilise a similar suspension arrangement as fitted to the Lotus Twelve Formula 2 racing car with two top and bottom wishbones, the front arm of the top wishbone acting as an anti-roll bar. Coil spring/damper units were fitted all round, the bottom of the rear struts picking up with the hub carrier. Initially, Chapman planned to use a British Motor Corporation (BMC) live rear axle but this was discarded in favour of double-jointed drive shafts which featured inboard disc brakes with trailing arm links to provide fore and aft location of the suspension unit.

The next stage was to transform the two-dimensional drawings into a $\frac{1}{5}$ scale model, a job which was given to the talented John Frayling whose interpretation gave the right degree of curves to produce a model everyone agreed upon. Stylist John Frayling was working for Ford at the time and had met Colin through a colleague, Ron Hickman — another talented designer from the antipodes who was working at Dagenham. Hickman was also free-lancing for a Fleet Street publishing house when he was invited onto the Lotus stand at the 1955 Motor Show. A chance remark brought forth an invitation to meet Chapman the following Saturday at a Hornsey hostelry. Hickman took along Frayling and another talented person from the Ford Design Studio, Peter Cambridge, whose speciality was styling automotive interiors.

John Frayling

Born in Poverty Bay, New Zealand where he spent his early life, John Frayling was the man who contributed much over the years to the style of Lotus cars, his last-minute adjustments often being all that was needed to turn a good shape into a brilliant one.

For family reasons, John moved to the UK while still a young man and began attending art school in central London. This training was to hone his eye for line and form — something which would be so crucial in his work for Chapman. Marriage meant the responsibilities of a steady job and after seeing an advertisement for a position with Ford he applied.

As a member of Ford's Styling Studios he soon learned about the meeting which had been arranged between Ron Hickman and Colin Chapman, and John and another Ford designer, Peter Cambridge, were asked to go along. The result of that meeting was that with the Elite programme coming on stream, John decided to give up his job with Ford and concentrate on the project at Lotus. He worked closely with Peter Kirwan-Taylor to produce first the scale models, then the full-size models used to develop the body moulds.

With the Elite programme completed, John then began looking at the Elan but decided to go free-lance. After producing only the first few proposals he left Ron Hickman to complete the task. Meanwhile, John became the styling consultant Chapman would always call in to advise — and invariably improve — upon designs which were created for new models. This function he continued to fulfil until Chapman's death in 1982. 'The point about designers is that they never stop designing,' says John.

John Frayling who started the work of fashioning the Elite clay model and who over the years contributed a great deal to Lotus's designs.

One of the two models had semi-shrouded wheelarches similar to those on the Lotus Eleven. These were clearly not liked and the next model featured the round wheelarches of the final production car.

SECRET DEVELOPMENTS

1956 was proving to be a busy year so, with space at the Tottenham Lane site at a premium, Chapman took over a small factory at nearby Edmonton where work on the Elite could begin away from prying eyes. The next job was to produce a set of scale drawings of the exquisite little model, the dimensions of which could then be enlarged and used to make a series of wooden sectional formers

'I would describe Kirwan-Taylor's role in the Elite saga as that of Design Manager,' recalled John Frayling. 'I did two ⅕ scale models for the Elite which were produced in modelling clay and reinforced with balsawood and we went to see Chapman with these models tucked under our arms.'

formers which would profile the shape of the car at intervals along its length. The formers were then covered with a mesh of chicken wire which formed the basis for the plaster of Paris which was spread like marmalade on top. Then, using hand tools, the final shape of the full-size body was created.

Inevitably, this aspect of the job was the most intricate and time-consuming although it is here that Chapman was immensely lucky in having the creative talent of Frayling on hand to undertake this very detailed work. Albert Adams, now Head of Composites at Lotus, recalled this period in the slow evolution of the Elite's programme:

'I have fond memories of working with John on the Elite's plaster model, John with his shirt sleeves rolled up and no shoes or socks on. His hairy arms would be completely covered in this white mess, to say nothing of his feet. When we adjourned for lunch, the local restaurant became very annoyed and almost banned John from coming in because of the trail of white footprints he left everywhere.'

To ensure that the overall surface of the cast was smooth and free from imperfections, it was given a coat of black paint. Eventually, the team were satisfied with the result and called Chapman on the phone. He took one look and said straight away, 'That's fantastic . . . We'll have it finished in time for the London Show.' This was just over two months away! (In fact, Chapman had hoped that the Elite would be finished in time for the 1957 Le Mans and entry procedures had been put in hand although, clearly, this plan was a little too ambitious.)

Since the Elite was to be – by Lotus standards anyway – a mass-produced model, it was clear from the beginning that the labour intensive process of manufacturing the beautifully-finished racing car bodies could not be used on the Elite. But what was the alternative? The solution was

glass reinforced plastic (GRP), a material which had been perfected in the States for producing the hulls for pleasure boats. It neatly overcame the problem of making compound shapes of considerable strength, eliminating the need for costly tooling. In his usual thorough and logical way, Chapman investigated this revolutionary material, reading handbooks and listening to experts. With his structural engineering background, he realised that by careful design a shell could be produced using GRP which would actually be strong enough to accept a vehicle's suspension units, so long as the correct stressing was accounted for. But then Chapman had already demonstrated this admirably with his sports/racing cars with their lightweight spaceframe chassis. GRP it had to be!

As for a suitable power unit, by the time Chapman began considering what engine he could use, his relationship with Coventry–Climax had matured nicely. He had already used their 1,098cc FWA engine as well as the 1,460cc FWC unit, both of which had proved reliable and powerful, if extremely costly. The difficulty was that Chapman wanted an engine with a capacity as close as possible to 1,300cc so that it would be competitive in the 1,300cc Grand Touring Class. To commission Coventry–Climax to design and build an all-new engine would be out of the question. The solution was to combine the 67.3mm stroke of the FWA engine with the 76.2mm bore of the FWB; the resultant 1,216cc engine, while special to the Elite, was at least assembled from existing components. This engine became known as the FWE unit and produced 75bhp at 6,100rpm. The compression was set at 8.5:1 and it utilised a single 1.5in (3.81cm) SU carburettor. An 8in (20.32cm) BMC clutch transmitted the drive to an MGA-type gearbox which had synchromesh on the top three ratios. The 4.22:1 final drive, another BMC item, was located in a specially made Lotus alloy casting. Since Chapman had opted to use BMC parts there was the

Just nine years separate the Lotus Eleven and the design of the Elan which was introduced in 1963.

benefit of other final drive ratios available.

Meanwhile, the team at Edmonton were feverishly working to meet Chapman's self-imposed completion date of October 1957 when the car was to be seen for the first time by the public. The interior design came under the control of Peter Cambridge. Here again, it needed the talents of someone used to creating the kind of trim and dashboard style which buyers of road sports cars had come to expect rather than the austerity feel of a race car. The result was a simple yet tasteful dashboard which, in profile, almost reflected the Elite's silhouette. The seats were sub-contracted to Cox & Co. Ltd. of Watford who produced a high-backed design with just the right amount of support to hold the occupants in position while enjoying the Elite's outstanding roadholding.

With the final mock-up completed the Elite body master could be made. This aspect of the job became somewhat prolonged because the final shell was made up from a total of sixty mouldings which then had to be fitted together like a jigsaw. In fact, time got so short that the trimmer had to continue working inside the car while the shell was given its coats of two-tone grey paint!

'We all learnt a great deal in those early days,' Frayling continued. 'When we did the initial styling for the Elite we gave no thought as to how we would actually go about moulding these complex shapes.'

Like many specialist manufacturers before and since, Chapman's impatience to have his car on display was rewarded by a large order book which, in turn, led to customers having a frustrating wait before production actually began. First on the list of areas to be pro-duction engineered was the reduction of the number of body sections from sixty to three (the main body-shell itself; an inner skin which entailed the interior panels, engine bay walls and transmission tunnel; and a third unit which formed the entire floor pan with front and rear wheelarch panels). In addition were the bonnet, boot lid and doors.

John Frayling had already made a start on the Elite body and, unbeknown to Chapman, had introduced the idea of double-skinned GRP panels which created two smooth outer surfaces, but valuable time was being spent in an effort to perfect the technique. So, Ron Hickman left Ford to join John working for Lotus full-time.

'John had lost his way' explained Hickman, 'and was disillusioned with the project. While it was too late to stop the double skinning idea for the body panels (which was a nightmare) I was able to organise the Elite into production.'

It is here that Chapman's true genius can be appreciated. His calculations were based on eight major stress boxes within the body which would accommodate the tensions imposed by the installation of the suspension and drivetrain, these boxes being along each sill section, one on each side to create the scuttle, one to form the transmission tunnel, one to form the body interior, one to form the air duct in the nose section and finally one to form the final drive location. Square-section metal tubes were bonded into the centre body moulding around the scuttle area to provide added stiffness and anchorage for the door hinges as well as providing the essential strength for jacking points beneath. And a hoop framework was added around the windscreen to give added protection.

LOTUS BLOSSOMS

After its successful appearance at the London Show, the first Elite prototype was broken up and plans made to build a batch of ten further prototypes in the Edmonton workshop. These cars were earmarked for Lotus agents and for racing, the feedback on how they performed providing vital information before production proper got into high gear. However, if time was being lost getting the Elite into production, a far more serious problem had yet to be resolved – that of finding somewhere to build a new factory. The combined activities of manufacturing the existing range of Lotus products (the Seven and the Eleven) and the development and manufacture of tuning parts, left precious little space for the Elite, despite the recent additions at Tottenham Lane and the Edmonton premises.

'While I wasn't able to evaluate the team's technical ability' said Fred Bushell, 'I was impressed by their enthusiasm. There were people at Lotus like Graham Hill, Keith Duckworth and Mike Costin who were of the calibre that they could quite easily have gone

off and done something different. So I told Colin I wanted three months to wind-up my affairs and I finally joined him in August 1958.'

The first Elite to be tested under power was taken to Brands Hatch for trials. Fitted with an 1,100cc version of the Coventry – Climax engine, it was a left-hand drive car which was due to be exhibited later at the Geneva Show. Initial reaction to the way the car performed was favourable. Fred Bushell continued:

'On my first day at Lotus I was confronted by a jubilant Chapman who had just signed a contract to have a new factory built at Cheshunt. I took one look at it and said that at the current build-rate there was no way he could afford the impressive structure on order. So Colin did no more than call the

The Elite on display at the 1960 Earls Court Show. The concept of its sleek shape was the work of Peter Kirwan-Taylor.

LOTUS ELITE

Approximately 1,000 were built between May 1958 and March 1964; chassis numbers were from EC1001.

Engine
Four-cylinder
Cubic capacity   1,216cc
Bore and stroke   76.2mm × 66.7mm
Maximum power   72bhp at 6,200rpm (with single 1.5in (3.8cm) SU carburettor) or 83bhp at 6,300rpm (with optional twin 1.5in (3.8cm) SUs)
Maximum torque   77lb ft at 3,800rpm
Compression ratio   10:1
Also available with optional twin 40DCOE Weber carburettors, giving approximately 100bhp.

Chassis
Weight (on road)   1,480lb (671.33kg)
Wheelbase   7ft 4.25in (2.24m)
Front track   3ft 11in (1.19m)
Rear track   4ft 0.25in (1.26m)
Length   12ft 4in (3.76m)
Width   4ft 11.25in (1.5m)
Height   3ft 10.5in (1.18m)
Turning circle   37ft 10in (11.53m)
Front suspension   Independent, wishbones on coil springs, Armstrong telescopic dampers, anti-roll bar
Rear suspension   Independent Chapman strut, radius arms
Brakes   9.5in discs all round
Gearbox
Four-speed − overall ratios with 4.22:1 rear axle
　　1st gear   4.22
　　2nd gear   5.80
　　3rd gear   9.34
　　4th gear   15.29
　　reverse   20.09
Optional MG close ratio
　　1st gear   4.22
　　2nd gear   5.56
　　3rd gear   7.39
　　4th gear   10.33
　　reverse   20.09
Optional ZF
　　1st gear   4.22
　　2nd gear   5.16
　　3rd gear   7.18
　　4th gear   10.62
　　reverse   10.87
3.7:1, 4.55 and 4.875 rear axle ratios optional
Steering   rack and pinion
Wheels and tyres   15in × 4.8in wires all round

builder back into his office, introduced me to him and said I'd got something to say. The builder was enormous, he almost filled Colin's office. Anyway, I said there was no way we could afford the factory as it was. Naturally, the builder was very annoyed but eventually we were able to placate him and pare it down to something within our reach.'

From the complicated tubular chassis of the Eleven, Lotus designers produced a sheet steel backbone chassis which gave the Elan outstanding handling.

Fundamental to the financing of the Cheshunt factory were the paper sales of the Elite. Demand was strong on both sides of the Atlantic and Fred was able to arrange letters of credit which were sufficient to underwrite the manufacture of 600 cars. Based on this, work began on the new plant with Elite production actually starting in mid-1959. In fact, there were few changes between the prototype cars and the production Elites. Technically, the original proposal for bonding metal plates into the GRP at suspension and engine attachment points was cancelled in favour of thicker GRP with rubber mountings. Also, the engine mountings were moved upwards and rearwards while the cooling system was fitted with a thermostatically controlled electric fan. As for the interior, production Elites were trimmed to a far better standard than the prototype cars in line with their Grand Tourer image.

Manufacture of the GRP bodies was subcontracted to a small firm of marine laminators, Maximar of Pulborough, West Sussex. The moulds were transported to the company although in the early days, Ron Hickman, John Frayling and Albert Adams often had to go down to Sussex and work on the Elite moulds in an effort to get production on stream. The Elite's production programme called for the combined body chassis units to be delivered to the Cheshunt factory fully finished and trimmed. However, in view of Lotus's lack of experience with series production and the differences between laying up boat hulls and the Elite's delicately balanced shape, it's hardly surprising that there were snags. Worse still, this revolutionary material called GRP which was supposed to be the low volume manufacturer's salvation, had a mind of its own unless the person laying up the mould knew what he was about. Care had to be taken over letting the mould cure otherwise uneven drying caused problems. Quality control was a nightmare. Despite efforts on both sides, Chapman was aware that he had to act quickly to retrieve the situation.

The solution was to cancel the contract with Maximar and move the work to the Bristol Aircraft Company, makers of the

When compared to the Elite the interior of the Elan was positively luxurious with its veneer dashboard and washable vinyl seats and trim.

The steel wheels seen on this Elan look positively skinny when compared to the wide wheels and low profile tyres fitted to comtemporary sports cars.

The dashboard arrangement of the Elite was functional – as one might expect from Lotus – and this theme was carried over to the Elan.

quality Bristol car. Bristol already had a high reputation in the automotive and aeronautical worlds and indeed, had supplied Lotus with their 2-litre engines for use in the Lotus X racing car, sister to the sleek Lotus Eleven which had gained such favourable publicity throughout the racing world. Between the latter part of 1959 and mid-1960 Bristol took the opportunity to make the necessary preparations for undertaking the precise job of the manufacture of the Elite body/chassis.

ENTER THE SERIES 2

Meanwhile, Lotus were busily making alterations to the Series 1 car, which included modifying the rear of the seats to take the lift-out side windows, changing to a cable-operated throttle and modifying the handbrake location to a position under the dashboard. In typical Chapman fashion, the opportunity for extra publicity from sub-contracting the manufacture of the Elite bodies to such a prestigious firm as Bristol was not allowed to escape. Moreover, to pacify the critics, a handful of additional modifications were made, the most significant being the alteration of the rear suspension arrangement which involved changing the strut locating links in an effort to overcome rear wheel swing, a nasty experience when cornering at speed! Also, the spring rates were reduced to give the car a softer ride and the Firestone tyres were

The functional interior of the Elite. It was Lotus's first volume production car and the company had a great deal to learn about manufacturing a road sports car.

John Threfall at the wheel of an Elite at Silverstone in late 1961. Lotus's first 'volume' production car, the Elite, proved to be very competitive on the tracks.

And this was the reason why the Elite was so costly to make — its unique version of the race-bred Coventry—Climax engine. The Elan's Ford-based unit was much cheaper to make.

With the introduction of the Elan, Lotus began laying up their sports car bodies using GRP thereby making them easy and cheap to produce and immune to rust.

replaced by Michelin X or Pirelli radials. The car was referred to as the Series 2.

Yet more improvements were in store as the Series 2 got on stream. The clutch system was given a larger slave cylinder to reduce pedal pressure, while the steering wheel was now a thicker, 15in (38.1cm) type. Subtle changes were made to the interior trim, too. However, by far the greatest shortcoming of the Elite as an elegant road car for the connoisseur was the level of interior noise. At the outset, a serious oversight in the car's overall composition was that the fibreglass body sections acted as sound boxes, the material resonating to the frequencies of the engine, exhaust and road noises. No matter what lengths were taken to add sound-deadening material to the interior, the problem persisted for the Elite's lifetime.

Naturally, the Elite attracted a great many enthusiasts who liked to enter club events at the weekend. For those customers Lotus offered a Special Equipment version which

was launched at the 1960 Show. The SE's engine featured a high-lift camshaft, twin 1.5in (3.81cm) SU carburettors and a four-branch exhaust manifold, all of which increased the power output to 85bhp. The BMC gearbox was replaced by a Lotus-built unit with ZF internals which had the bonus of synchromesh on all forward gears. However, as Elite sales began to slip because of its high retail price, a Lotus dealer named David Buxton started offering his own special versions of the Elite known as the Super 95, 100 and 105. These cars were marketed from mid-1962. The 95 was offered in essentially Special Equipment tune, the 100 with a five-bearing crankshaft and 10.5:1 compression ratio, and the 105 with twin Weber carburettors. Also included in the specifications were long-range fuel tanks, servo brakes and a bonnet scoop.

By the time Elite production gave way to the cheaper Elan there were some thirty or so body-shells remaining and a programme was

The Elan Sprint was the last Elan to be produced although some enthusiasts still maintain the earlier Elite was the prettier car.

planned to fit Elan running gear beneath these last shells. However, Chapman was unhappy with the result and cancelled the project. A further prototype with revised specification was tested by *Car* but by then the Elan was too well established.

In financial terms, the Elite returned an overall loss due largely to the high cost of the Coventry–Climax engine. Moreover, while it must have been very gratifying for Lotus to see so many of their cars being exported to the States, poor reliability and quality caused a great many warranty claims. The situation was compounded by the fact that the American distributor and Lotus were not on the best of terms. The situation gradually deteriorated and it was left to Fred Bushell to sort things out. At one point Fred even found himself looking down the blade of the American distributor's knife-wielding minder! Elite sales in the UK were never quite like this.

2 Elan Makes its Mark

While the buying public may have been surprised by the beauty of the Elite (especially as it had been designed by such a small company), as far as Lotus were concerned their first attempt at marketing a sports coupe had cost them dearly. Rumour has it that of the 1,000 or so cars that were made during the period 1958–1963 (the first two Elites were delivered on 31 December 1958: one to band leader Chris Barber, the other to Ian Scott-Watson) Lotus lost around £100 per car. Clearly, in view of how well the Elite was accepted, this was a tragedy and it was to plunge the company into a period of financial difficulty. Not until the Elan became established did Lotus's monetary position regain a degree of stability. However, part of the Chapman genius was that he was able to learn by his mistakes. While the previous model influenced the design of the next, so too did its shortcomings. The Elite's successor had to be fast, attractive, able to handle well and above all else, *profitable*. It had to be a car that could be built and repaired quickly (Lotus were still smarting from the American warranty claims on the Elite). It had to be 'productionised'. It was also going to be an open car.

An early photograph of Colin Chapman in characteristic pose with stop-watch in hand. Compare this to the picture of him in Chapter 9.

CUTTING COSTS

When preparing the specification for the new car the most obvious area where costs could be cut was that of buying in a more economically-priced power unit. The FWE Coventry–Climax engine alone accounted for nearly twenty-five per cent of the total cost of the Elite, the penalty of using a low volume specialist engine. An example of the complete opposite was the little Austin–Healey Sprite which utilised the mass-

The Elite was an elegant looking car yet it was expensive to build. In designing the Elan, Lotus were adamant that it would be profitable for the company.

produced BMC 'A' series engine. This little sports car was unveiled to the public in mid-1958, just six months before the first Elites left Cheshunt. Whether Donald Healey's Sprite actually influenced Chapman is hard to say. However, its concept was food for thought . . .

Another area where costs could be substantially cut was the choice of suspension units. The Elite's front wishbone set-up was special to the Lotus. However, Triumph's new Herald family saloon featured a simple yet effective double-wishbone arrangement manufactured from stamped pressings with coil spring/damper units and steering was provided by an Alford and Alder rack-and-pinion system. Better still, Triumph were developing the Herald with front disc brakes. The rear suspension proved a little more of a problem. (Anyway, Chapman wanted to incorporate a little original thinking.) It had to

be independent, but Chapman had an aversion to cheaply-made splined shafts. (The splines themselves, he argued, tend to lock up under driveshaft plunge/power-on conditions.) His answer was to use Metalastik rubber couplings which interfaced driveshaft movement with the fixed drive line of the differential – simple yet effective. Disc brakes were fitted with coil spring/dampers while the hub location was taken care of by large 'A' frame wishbones.

Equally, Chapman was anxious to continue to put into practice his theories on the use of GRP in the manufacture of bodies, which were specially designed so that, as in the Elite, there was sufficient strength to eliminate the need for a separate chassis. Despite the relative complexity of the Elite's three-section shell, Chapman was still convinced that it was possible to manufacture bodies in one piece with the necessary

Ron Hickman

A South African born in 1932, Ron spent six years in a magistrates office after matriculating. A life-long ambition to become involved with designing cars encouraged him to move to the UK. However, on his arrival in England he began working for the music publishers, Boosey & Hawkes.

He then joined Ford's Styling Studios. Having already been commissioned to write and illustrate a feature on the London Motor Show for a South African magazine, he took time off from Ford and went along to the Show where he met Lotus's Press Officer. This conversation led to a meeting being arranged between Ron Hickman and Colin Chapman. As a result, Ron (like so many other enthusiasts) began moonlighting for Lotus, helping to design the moulds for the Elite. Later, he left Ford to productionise the Elite and went on to work on the Elan and +2, his engineering and design talents being invaluable to these projects.

However, by 1967 Hickman decided to leave Lotus and joined a furniture design company. Later still, he moved to Jersey having had the satisfaction of seeing his brainchild, the Workmate, become a household name.

Hickman says he looks back on his period with Lotus as being a most exciting time in his life, learning at perhaps five times the rate he would have normally. 'There was never a better time to have joined,' he recalls.

Ron Hickman, designer and Project Engineer for the Lotus Elan.

Anglia. As a study in engine design its main attribute was that its proportions — 31.87in × 19.06in (80.96cm × 48.41cm) — were very 'over square'. The unit developed an unstressed 39bhp at 5,000 rpm and the attraction for the engine tuners was that its bore/stroke ratio meant that it could take high compression ratios and wild camshaft profiles without complaint.

BODY-BUILDING THE ELAN

The job of perfecting the design of the body so that it had the required strength for an open sports car was the responsibility of Ron Hickman. However, even this talented engineer could not overcome the lack of rigidity created by the absence of a roof

integral strength a body/chassis monocoque demanded. As Albert Adams confirmed, even at this early stage Lotus were increasing their GRP moulding experience and Colin was thinking of ways in which ready-painted bodies could be lifted straight from the mould.

1958 had another significance in the evolution of the Elan for it was then that Ford introduced their new four-cylinder 998cc ohv engine (code named 105E) which was fitted into a two-door saloon car called the Ford

A Series 4 Elan showing its sleek bonnet line and integral
bumper which was a novel feature developed by Ron Hickman.

The first pop-up headlights fitted to
Elans were raised using vacuum
assistance. Unfortunately, when the
throttle was opened the headlights
would disappear into the body

The 'Elan' badge as fitted to a Series
4 Elan soft-top.

section. Furthermore, there was even the possibility at this stage that the car would not be a 1-litre model at all but a 100 (or so) bhp 1.5-litre — which would place even greater emphasis on the need to produce a monocoque strong enough to handle the extra power.

'Initially, the idea of the Elan was that it should be a replacement for the Lotus Seven. I did a few styling proposals, although at that stage the Elan's concept was that it should be a monolithic construction in which the GRP body sections were stuck together while they were still wet' explained John Frayling. 'At the time I left the company, the idea of using a separate backbone chassis hadn't been

thought of and Ron Hickman and his team made a great many changes before the Elan reached production.'

During a British Racing Sports Car Club (BRSCC) dinner Ron broached the subject with Chapman. The result of this conversation was a design for a backbone-type chassis frame manufactured from sheet steel panels folded at right angles and attached to form a narrow aspect figure 'X'. A prototype chassis was quickly assembled to act as a test bed for the suspension design and a Falcon glass-fibre body mounted on to it. Power was provided by the newly-launched Ford engine so that the car could be used for testing. After many thousands of miles of testing it became

An early scale model of a proposal for the Elan. At this stage the styling appears to be a mixture of Elite and Austin–Healey Sprite.

clear that the folded steel chassis really did give the car great torsional rigidity. It also considerably reduced rattles and vibration from body flexing. However, the driveshaft doughnuts, good though they were, tended to twist severely under braking. The solution was to improve the location of the differential mounting and the rear disc brakes were moved outboard on to the wheel hubs. However, with the backbone chassis having such an effect on the car's road manners, it was decided to put it to the test and, with the car dismantled, it was found to have an impressive 600lb ft of strength per degree of applied twist. Since this was a prototype chassis it had been built with no special consideration for weight. But the concept was obviously so right for what was needed to give the car its desired rigidity. A less weighty frame would supply the required strength.

Fundamental to the final design of the backbone chassis was that the structure should be strong enough to handle the stresses imposed under enthusiastic driving, yet be light enough with no excess metal anywhere. After exhaustive tests a final twist figure of 4,300lb ft per degree was decided upon, the main chassis sections being fabricated from 18SWG sheet steel with thinner 16SWG plates attached to it for strengthening. The centre section of the structure was top-hat shaped in profile and formed the transmission tunnel, which the prop shaft would pass through. 6in (15.24cm) wide and 11.5in (29.21cm) deep, it was this section which absorbed the main stresses of the entire chassis. From this centre unit, four chassis legs splayed out fore and aft to pick up with each wheel, the engine and gearbox being placed between the front legs and the differential between the rear legs. Suspension turrets, again formed from sheet steel panels, were attached at all four corners to carry the coil spring/damper units. It was an ingenious and cost-effective concept and one which would be used on all future road-going Lotus models.

POWER PROBLEMS

As for the problem over which power unit to use, like so many of the problems Chapman encountered in his designs, the solution was provided by one of his business contacts. In this case, the contact was Walter Hayes, whom Chapman had met while Hayes was working for the *Sunday Dispatch*. By the late 1950s Hayes had moved on to become public relations supremo at Ford. During a meeting with Chapman, Hayes outlined Ford's future engine development programme which involved a family of ohv engines, based on an 'over-square' design, starting with a 997cc unit and on to 1,200cc, 1,340cc and finally 1,500cc variants. Clearly, the Ford engines would cost Chapman considerably less than the very expensive Coventry–Climax units. However, even in 1,500cc form the Ford engine would not develop anything like the power Chapman had in mind for his new sports car. Any successor to the lithe Elite would have to be at least as quick. Manufacturing costs of the new car would mean that its retail price would be such that it *had* to be impressively fast – a 90mph (144.8kph) Lotus just was not acceptable.

It must be said at this point that Chapman had at one time run a Ford Consul (yes, really) with a Raymond May's cylinder head, the conversion vastly improving its performance. However, it is hardly likely that Chapman gave much serious thought to applying this kind of answer to increasing the power output of a standard Ford engine since the technical specification was simply not impressive enough for the average Lotus customer. It did, however, give him food for thought. Chapman's answer was to utilise the main components from the new range of Ford engines, replacing the ohv cylinder head with a specially designed twin camshaft version similar in concept to the six-cylinder Jaguar XK engine. But, who would undertake the work of designing the head?

Despite their almost crude appearance, the seats in the Elan always came in for praise from the motoring magazines.

In fact, Chapman's concept of utilising the main components from the Ford engine and adding a special tohc cylinder head neatly tied in with Hayes's own plans for promoting Ford through a programme of motor sport which would involve marketing a high performance version of the soon-to-be-released Cortina saloon. Ford would supply the cars and Lotus would modify them, fitting Chapman's tohc engine. The deal not only brought the two companies closer together, it would also provide much needed revenue when the car reached the showrooms as the Lotus Cortina. However, that was still a long way off and relations between the two companies would become strained before production got under way.)

Again, Chapman made use of a contact he had made, someone on one of the main motoring journals: Harry Mundy. At the time, the multi-talented Mundy was working

as Technical Editor on the staff of *Autocar*, although he had spent some time working as Chief Designer at Coventry−Climax. Chapman's proposal was that Mundy should prepare the concept for the tohc cylinder head.

Initially, Mundy's design was for use on either the 997cc or 1,340cc Ford engines. Basically, the block, crankshaft, rods and pistons from the Ford engine would be retained, along with the old camshaft (since this drove the oil pump and distributor jackshaft), but the ohv cylinder head would be replaced by a tohc head driven by a single timing chain. Although retaining the flat-topped Ford pistons created a problem for the opposed inlet and exhaust valves, Mundy ingeniously overcame this by making the valve angle as shallow as possible − 27° in fact. Stories of Mundy accepting the project in return for a £1 royalty on each engine sold or a cash sum (which he accepted) are now legendary, although it must be considered that if Mundy was asked to design an engine initially for racing (it was raced first at the Nurburgring) he probably thought sales would not be that high.

The man mainly responsible for transposing Mundy's design work into detail drawings was Richard Ansdale, an engineer working for Thorneycroft. Ansdale, moonlighting as people so often did for Lotus, produced the engineering drawings and the design for a new water pump as it was no longer possible to use the original Ford part because Mundy's head protruded beyond the front face of the cylinder block. Apart from the old Ford water pump bearing, the rest was new. At this point the job of actually making the components was brought in-house and given to Steve Sanville who calculated the assembly dimensions and took the drawings to a costing pattern maker in East London. The patterns were then sent to Birmid who cast the first of the tohc cylinder heads and two-part timing chain cover. Fitted to a 105E 997cc block, the engine was reckoned to produce around 85bhp.

By late 1961 more development work was being done with three bearing 1,100cc versions of this engine and a 1,477cc unit. Inevitably, as these were prototype units, there were problems with head gasket and main bearing failures. Undeterred, the engines were rebuilt and a left-hand drive ex-Embassy Ford Anglia saloon was bought, modified with disc brakes and pressed into service as a development hack. Mike Costin (who by this time had set up Cosworth Engineering Limited with Keith Duckworth, but who still had some time left before his contract with Lotus expired) took one of the prototype heads to Harry Weslake for gas flow analysis. The design was such that little alteration was needed.

As 1961 gave way to 1962, Chapman and his team began giving some thought to the assembly of the new engines. The company's position was becoming desperate as the high retail price of the Elite caused sales to slump. The cost of the Cheshunt factory had further weakened the company's finances so they were in no position to consider building the engines themselves. Several companies were approached about taking on the work. Finally, JA Prestwich of Tottenham agreed to accept the contract.

In mid-1962 Ford launched their 1,500cc version, thereby completing the family of engines Walter Hayes had discussed with Chapman earlier. Lotus immediately took delivery of a cylinder block and used it as the foundation for another prototype engine. This, and a 1,477cc engine, were taken to Nurburgring where the 1.5-litre engine was fitted in a Lotus 23. In a dramatic performance Jim Clark outstripped the opposition, which included a 3-litre Ferrari, demonstrating convincingly the capabilities of the new tohc Lotus engine. Production of the engine, however, was still some way off. In the meantime, Keith Duckworth built two 1,500cc engines for Lotus 23 racing cars and continued development of the tohc engine for racing.

In October 1962, JA Prestwich were given the contract to begin production of the 1,500cc tohc engine for the new Lotus sports car and later that month the first production specification engine was run up on its test bed. With the delightful backbone chassis now tested and agreed, Ron Hickman and his team turned their attention to the body styling. Not surprisingly, Chapman was becoming very concerned about costs and Hickman was instructed to utilise as many cheap mass-produced components as possible in its design. In view of the input from such gifted people as Peter Kirwan-Taylor and Frank Costin, the styling of the M2 (as the new sports car was coded) had nothing like the same attention.

'I think Chapman felt the first styling proposals for the Elan made it into a bit of an ugly duckling when compared to the Elite,' recalled Albert Adams, who joined Lotus as a young man in the mid-1950s. 'There were quite a few changes made to improve its looks although today, of course, the Elan is considered to be a classic.'

When the mock-ups for the Elan had been finalised, Williams & Pritchard then produced the alloy bucks from which the body moulds were made. The Elan body was formed from two halves. The inner section consisted of the wheelarches, scuttle, transmission tunnel and boot floor. Attached to this was the outer section from the sills upwards: wings, front apron and the complete rear of the car. A metal framework

was bonded in around the door apertures to add rigidity.

THE STAR OF THE SHOW

In true Lotus brinkmanship the Elan, destined for exhibition at the London Show, only just made it – and even then it was not actually running. It had been another all-nighter for the team – the headlights, for example, were propped open because lack of time had precluded them from being connected. Launched as the Elan 1500 it was priced at a very reasonable £1,095 in kit form

The Elan on the Lotus stand at the 1963 Earls Court Show where it was unveiled with a 1,500cc version of the Lotus/Ford tohc engine: the legend was just beginning.

or £1,499 fully assembled. (The price tag on the last Elite was £2,000.) Unfortunately, while the car was an undoubted success with many customers placing orders on the spot, there was a snag: the Elan had not actually reached production at this stage so potential buyers would have to curb their impatience.

'The first Elan was a pretty basic car,' remembered Morris Dowton who was Production Foreman. 'The hood mechanism simply consisted of sticks which were put in place when the hood needed to be erected. Inside were rubber mats in place of carpets.'

Throughout late 1962 further testing and development work was carried out on the production engine in an effort to increase power and make the unit more reliable. A change in the rules of international events relating to engines increased the size from 1,500cc to 1,600cc. In order to take advantage of this, Ford agreed only to supply blocks where the manufacturing tolerances had resulted in a cylinder block with sufficient metal around the bores to allow JA Prestwich (JAP) to increase them to 1,558cc. (Standard 1mm overbore allowed under the regulations then created a full 1,600cc engine.)

By January the following year the first two production Elan 1600s were finished. However, the power output from the larger engine was still below that which had been achieved with the earlier prototype engines. Lotus were also experiencing problems with the quality of the sandcast cylinder heads produced by Birmid, so when William Mills (another metal casting company) quoted just £2,000 for making patterns to produce the heads by die-casting, Chapman lost no time in accepting their offer.

Unfortunately, when the first engine which had been assembled by JAP using a Mills-made head was delivered to Cheshunt in late February it was found incapable of retaining its coolant. Further deliveries were made but at one point only twenty per cent

of the heads were found to be acceptable. The situation was becoming critical. Mills were contacted and asked politely but firmly to use sandcasting processes with the result that the failure rate was drastically reduced. With an improved quality of head gasket and modifications made to improve the rigidity of the cylinder head, William Mills continued to make the cylinder heads until Elan production ceased in 1973.

It was the job of JAP to machine the heads, fit the guides, valve springs and seats and then assemble them on to the blocks complete with crankshaft, rods and pistons which had arrived from Dagenham. Some eleven of the smaller 1,498cc versions of the tohc engines were built, mainly for testing and installation into the racing 23s, before production proper of the 1,558cc units came on stream in 1963 when the first soft-top Elan Series 1 began to hit the market place.

As work on the design of the body reached its final stages, other signs of the ingenuity of Ron Hickman could be identified. For example, the pop-up headlights, a Hickmanism to overcome the problems of maintaining the statutory height for headlamps without ruining the gracefully curved nose section of the bonnet. Hickman says he vividly recalls suggesting to Chapman that the headlights be mounted on pivoting pods, thinking that the great man would instantly dismiss the notion. In fact, Colin liked the idea and immediately solved the problem of how they should be powered by offering a scheme whereby the inlet manifold vacuum would make an ideal source of energy. (Unlike the wiper mechanisms of Ford's 1950s cars where excess use of the throttle caused the wipers to stop, in this case the vacuum was only being used once to force the light pods up – a very different matter.) Another example of Hickman's original thinking were the shaped bumpers which, like the headlight idea, were designs he had incorporated into a proposal for a sports car while working at Ford. Hickman's bumpers were so shaped

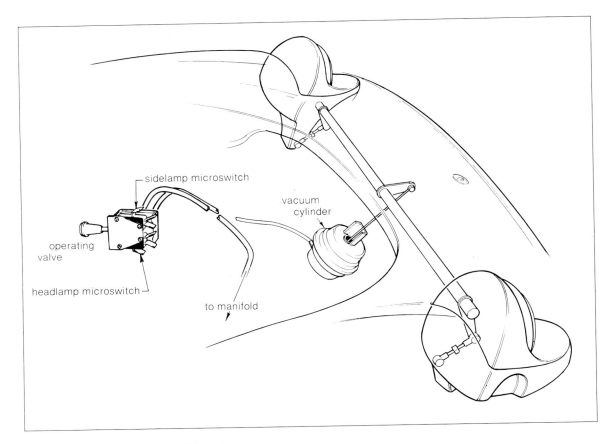

Headlamp vacuum system — fail-safe.

The interior of an S4 Elan with its rocker switches and new trim material for the seats. By 1968 the Elan was becoming affected by the emission and safety laws being introduced in America.

One of the reasons why the Elan became so popular as a touring car was the size of the boot which could accommodate a reasonable amount of luggage for two on holiday.

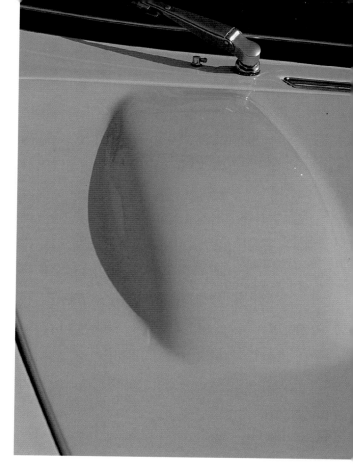

Steel wheels and chrome hub caps look out of place on a sports car. However, with the introduction of the Series 4, customers could specify knock-on wheels, which looked more sporty!

When the Weber carburettors were dropped in favour of the cheaper Stromberg units a bulge had to be incorporated into the bonnet. However, it was soon found that enthusiasts preferred the look of the Webers.

that they formed a continuation of the body line. Again, Chapman liked this novel approach of making the bumpers less obtrusive and approved their use on the new Elan. A considerable amount of time was spent developing a hood design which was capable of withstanding the buffeting of travelling at 100mph (160.9kph). The result was a GRP framework which ran on either side from the windscreen locating with the rear panel, two rails running across the car giving the hood its support when it was in place. When not in use, the complete hood assembly could be stored in the 5.9cu ft (0.17 cu m) boot.

While the Elite's interior trim quality was more than in keeping with its prestige image, from the outset the interior of the Elan was to

be functional, almost austere by comparison. The seats, which had been very costly items in the Elite, were to be simple, fixed-back chairs which would give hip-hugging support in a simple design. Lotus solved the problem of providing a comfortable position which was equally comfortable for both short and tall drivers by locating the seat on angled runners. If there was a weakness in the design of the interior it was the teak-trimmed facia. Ahead of the driver's eyeline were the usual twin gauges for revs and speed with fuel, oil and water state meters flanking them. In the centre was a position for a radio, while various knobs and switches were spread out below for activating wipers, lights and so on. To the left was an impressive-looking glove box. For left-hand drive cars, the layout pattern was simply reversed.

ELAN INTO HIGH GEAR

Elan production began in May 1963, a lengthy seven months after it had taken the world's motor press by storm at the previous year's London Show. Manufacture of the backbone chassis frame was farmed out to John Thompson in Wolverhampton while the GRP bodies were layed up in Lotus's own body shop at the end of Delamare Road in Cheshunt.

'We had four people working on one mould for body lay-ups,' recalled Tom Peters. 'By around 4.30 in the afternoon the shell had been finished and was put in an oven and the following morning it was checked over by the inspector. If he found any defects, the team then had to put them right. The main problem was that it was a seven-piece split mould.'

'When a laminator was about to lay up a certain part he'd go along to the foreman, explain which part he was about to make and the foreman would issue the resin and GRP in the ratio of 2.5 times resin to one part GRP and that would have to be sufficient for laying up that particular part,' recalled Bill Brown, who was on production assembly.

Fred Bushell recalled the early days of behind-the-scenes activities:

'The amusing thing about our meetings at Ford's headquarters was that there would be me and perhaps one other representative from Lotus sitting across the table from about twenty-five or so Ford executives. Even so, I think the reason Ford took us seriously was that by that time Cheshunt was up and running. People like Harley Copp and Walter Hayes had considerable influence and went to see the Cheshunt factory. Although, when compared to Ford, Lotus was very primitive, they could nevertheless see the level of Lotus's technical and management approach.'

Chapman, with his own personal mix of charm, flamboyancy, technical know-how and innovative talent, had managed to impress the Ford hierarchy although in late 1962 and early 1963 – with no cars to sell and the Lotus Cortina project stagnating too – even this might not have been sufficient to stave off a very nasty confrontation. Fortunately, production got under way just in time! The team – and Chapman in particular – must have heaved a sigh of relief when Lotus could begin to satisfy the clammering customers. In fact, the pressures simply to start the delivery ball rolling were such that less urgent matters (like productionising the nifty silver hardtop which had been seen on the London Show car in October 1962) were placed firmly on the back burner.

Meanwhile, despite the considerable experience which the development team had gained through production of the Elite, quality control was a daily problem which had to be faced. In the halcyon days of the Mark VI it was down to the customer how the car turned out. It was a basic car and customers who drove basic cars did not complain if the hood leaked, or the boot filled with water. It was all part of the *fun*. Suddenly, however, Lotus were faced with criticisms. Elan customers were a different breed. A committee was established to identify the ten worst faults and these included unsatisfactory action of the push-up side windows, water leaks, poor finish of facia, acid fumes from the cockpit-mounted battery, weak design of interior door handles and poor chroming on side window push-up handles, con rod failures and a final drive ratio which was too low to give relaxed high speed cruising.

ELAN SERIES 2

In November 1964 the Series 2 Elan was launched which largely overcame these problems. It featured a full-width veneer facia with a lockable glove box, chrome bezels to the dashboard instruments, Vauxhall Victor-type rear lamp cluster, larger front brake callipers, a quick release petrol filler cap (from the Sunbeam Alpine) and smaller foot pedals. It could also be ordered with optional centre-lock road wheels. The pop-up headlamp vacuum reservoir was made integral with the chassis frame and the battery – very sensibly – was relocated in the boot. Also, the comments concerning the poorly-designed manual window lifts and the interior door handles were overcome by redesigning them. However, a 3.55:1 final drive to overcome the complaints of the low axle ratio had to wait until the next series, although a novel modification which did

emerge on the Series 2 was a recalibrated oil pressure gauge which put the normal running pressure of 40psi further across the dial face, the needle thereby seeming to indicate a more robust pressure! As for technical changes, the cooling and fuel systems were modified, the latter to overcome the likelihood of fire. Also, in an acknowledgement of cars being sold to customers in hotter climates, the trim glue was changed to a less temperature-conscious variety. All in all, a very commendable list of modifications to engineer and install in such a short space of time.

Fred Bushell joined Lotus when the company was still at Hornsey, north London and was responsible for overseeing the company's early expansion.

Fred Bushell

For years, Fred Bushell was the management and financial wizard behind Lotus. A Londoner born in 1927, Fred completed his National Service and then undertook a three-year crash course in accountancy before joining Peat, Marwick, Mitchell & Company. However, a chance meeting in Hornsey with Colin Chapman was to alter his life and resulted in Fred joining Lotus in mid-1958.

He was the guiding hand behind many of Chapman's negotiations including, early on, sorting out the warranty claims on the Elite in the States. Fred was also behind the financing of the Cheshunt factory, as well as being deeply involved with the dealings with Ford over the purchase of parts during the Elan era. Later still came the setting up of arrangements to move the company to Norfolk and the deal which resulted in the tie-up between Lotus and Jensen over the Jensen–Healey sports car.

As Lotus moved into the 1980s Fred began spending more of his time at Ketteringham Hall, home of Team Lotus, where he became Chairman. Over the years, perhaps more than anyone else, Fred Bushell came to know the intimate workings of Lotus and the persona behind Colin Chapman. He joined Lotus thinking the company would not survive. 'It had no God-given right to,' Fred says, 'but I made sure it did.'

*A 1967 Elan coupe, which transformed the soft-top Elan into a
highly attractive sports tourer with such niceties as electric
windows and through-flow ventilation.*

Although late 1962 and early 1963 were breath-holding months for Lotus while they waited for the Elan to be put on stream, within a little over twelve months the pendulum of fortune swung towards Lotus once more. 1964 saw the Cheshunt team produce an impressive 1,762 units, of which 567 were the white and green Lotus Cortina saloons. It seemed that Chapman's dream of becoming a British Ferrari was back on course once more. Yet, despite the pressures (and even in the down period, too) there were light-hearted moments. The mini skirt was just becoming the height of fashion and whenever one of the office girls ventured out to walk along the first floor catwalk, she could always rely upon encouragement from the engineering staff below!

In view of the bold attempt to design and build the first Elan to a price limit, it soon became clear through Lotus Sales that there was a strong demand for a closed coupe, a successor to the exquisitely styled Elite. So, the gifted John Frayling turned his attention to styling a fixed roof for the Elan, with a shape which did not detract from the Elan's crisp, clean lines. He also modified the boot lid so that its lip extended over the edge of the rear transom panel.

Meanwhile, the engineering team were battling to reduce rattles and draughts. Feedback from the sales team called for a higher level of interior trim to include such niceties as electric windows, a 'proper' headlining and the latest type of heating and ventilation equipment. On the technical side, the list of improvements included the highly sought-after 3.7:1 final drive – a component lifted directly from the Ford Corsair – and the 2000E close ratio gearbox, another item taken from the 2-litre Corsair.

ELAN COUPE

Launched at the 1965 London Show the Elan Coupe caught the imagination of a whole new sector of the buying public. Moreover, invitations sent to a great many professional people to inspect the car on the Lotus stand further added to the interest and Lotus's order book was bulging once more. However, the through-flow ventilation system, another feature on the list of coupe attractions, had to wait a while because the men back at Cheshunt were still trying to perfect it!

Fred Bushell said it was probably characteristic of the man, but Chapman was always concerned with perfection of design. This meant he always found it difficult to freeze-frame a design and call it the Mark 1. 'Chapman' said Fred, 'always wanted to hold back — but then his perception of perfection was always changing. Meanwhile, I had the job of running the factory so that it paid wages each week!' Looking back, Fred said that the three production years 1962–65 were, pound-for-pound, the most profitable in the company's history.

Despite having extra land at Cheshunt on which to expand, the local authorities were not prepared to give the go-ahead for building. So, with history repeating itself, Chapman began looking elsewhere to relocate his business.

'I met Colin Chapman in the loo at the Savoy Hotel after the 1964 Lord Mayor's Show' recalled Tony Rudd, who later became Lotus's Engineering Director. ' "Just the bloke" said Chapman, "how'd you like to build competition twin-cam engines for Team Lotus?" Later, I introduced Colin to shooting and he

Like the front, the rear bumper was foam-filled GRP. The Elan was one of the first cars to have bumpers whose line followed the shape of the car.

came up to Norfolk where BRM had a test-track-cum-airfield. He arrived in the proto-type Elan +2 which I immediately thought was a very handsome car. He said he'd like to find somewhere like this. Later still, he told me he'd been offered a place in the Midlands and another at Hethel, although the local council at Hethel couldn't offer any incentives. "Forget the incentives," I told him. "Go for Hethel."'

Coincidentally, Lotus made the same gross profit that year (£400,000) as was needed to establish the new factory premises south west of Norwich.

ELAN SERIES 3

The thirst for greater performance was quenched by the launch of the Special Equipment convertible in January 1966. Steve Sanville and his team fitted new chokes and jets in the twin Weber carburettors, fitted the new high lift camshafts and then gave the cam covers a distinctive coat of paint. Power output was lifted to 115bhp, sufficient to produce a very acceptable 120mph (193.1kph) maximum speed. To tame this new-found potential performance, a servo unit was fitted to the brakes while the wheels were changed to a knock-off type. In fact, it was all something of a ploy to rejuvenate sales of the Series 2 drophead as the 'new' coupe-derived drophead had been delayed through problems with the hood, and engineering resources had been redirected to developing Chapman's latest development baby: the Elan +2.

Finally, it was ready and the Series 3 drophead hit the showrooms in June 1966 replacing the old Series 2 models. The new hood was certainly a neatly engineered unit. The hood canvas and frame could easily be folded back and covered by a tonneau, while it was quick to erect and the hood itself weatherproof. To aid sealing between the

side windows and the hood, the windows themselves were given metal surrounds. A month later a Special Equipment version of the Elan fhc (fixed-head coupe) was introduced, thereby giving the little car even more performance appeal.

LOTUS ON THE MOVE

From the beginning, it was clear that the little body-moulding factory was not going to be able to handle the throughput of shells once the Elan was on stream. A contract was therefore signed with a company called Bourne Plastics. However, meeting quality and production levels while trying to maintain costs within reasonable limits began to create real problems. Chapman therefore bought an old bedding factory at the end of Delamare Road in Cheshunt and, in typical Lotus high-gear fashion, in no time body mould production was transferred there and manufacture began in earnest. Naturally, there were rumours on the shop floor months in advance of the move to Norfolk. Finally, the entire staff were brought together for a meeting and, one Saturday morning, coaches stood by to ferry everyone (families included) to Norfolk for a look around Hethel and Norwich.

In order to get Hethel up and running, the body moulding shop was the first to be finished. The next stage was to set out the main assembly hall. Ivan Nollath and Bill Brown were two of the advance party who organised the layout of the main assembly hall at Hethel.

'This was the assembly and machine shop and, compared to what we'd been used to at Cheshunt, it was a very impressive building,' recalled Ivan as we stood in the very same building, now busily engaged in the assembly of Lotus Esprits and Esprit Turbos. 'Expenditure on equipment, though, was kept to a minimum. It was so large in here

The dashboard treatment of an Elan S4. Notice the small 'eyeball' ventilators at the extreme ends of the panel which were especially useful on the fixed-head version.

that during our free time while we were setting out the assembly lines we'd play football.'

The move from Cheshunt to Hethel was undertaken over a weekend. Memories among the staff of the cold November night when lorries from Cheshunt arrived loaded with Elan parts ready for production to begin in its new home the following morning are many and varied.

'The temperature was about −20°F (or it seemed like it, anyway) and before the Elan bodies were allowed into the new factory they were taken to the body shop and sprayed by the light of a Tilley lamp,' recalled Ivan.

'Somehow we managed,' said Albert Adams. 'Don't forget, at that time we were making 125 cars per week − a level we've never reached since − and to maintain that level

while changing locations was indeed quite a feat.'

Rumour has it, though, that in the move to Hethel some fifty twin-cam engines never completed the journey. One can only hope they were not damaged as they fell from the moving lorry!

The move to Hethel also coincided with changes to the assembly pattern of the twin-cam engines. JAP were taken over by Norton and Lotus engine assembly was moved to Wolverhampton. This situation, though, was far from ideal. So, in mid-1967 twin-cam engine assembly was removed from Wolverhampton and established at Hethel, where it remained. With the introduction of the Mark II Cortina, Ford took the opportunity to begin making the Lotus Cortina in-house; the car then becoming the Cortina−Lotus!

An Elan S4 drophead which was introduced in 1968. By this time assembly of the Lotus/Ford tohc engine had been moved to Hethel.

Pop-up style headlights gave both the
Elan and the larger Elan +2 a sleek
frontal appearance, although they
hardly looked elegant when in the
operated position.

An Elan S4 badge. By the
introduction of this model in 1968
production at Hethel was really
getting into high gear with some 125
cars coming off the line each week.

The interior of a late model Elan. With the introduction of this
car, Lotus quickly learned the science of interior trimming
which was a dramatic improvement over the Elite.

ELAN SERIES 4

In addition to the detail design work which would form the updates for the Series 4 Elan, the energetic engine development team under Steve Sanville began work on extracting more power from the road-going version of the 1,558cc twin-cam engine. Five years on from the Elan's introduction it was decided to produce a specification which raised power output but without great expense being incurred in changes to its major components. A set of uprated camshafts tuned to larger jets and chokes in the Webers and a different ignition setting topped off with a higher compression ratio of 10.3:1 increased power to 124bhp. Called the Super S/E engine, performance of a Series 3 development car fitted with one of these pepped-up units made the car really hum. But at the same time it showed up the Elan's drivetrain weakness − the Rotaflex coupling in the half-shafts. It was for this reason that this engine was never productionised.

The Series 4 Elan was launched at the 1968 London Motor Show. It featured a number of changes which were becoming mandatory under the new emission and safety laws that were becoming all the rage in the States. Rocker-type switches were let into the facia and the steering column was changed to a collapsible version. In addition, there were larger rear light clusters, flared wheelarches (to accept the 155 × 13in low-profile tyres), a twin-pipe exhaust and new trim for the seats. A short time after the Show, Lotus's MD Denis Austin happened to remark to Chapman that the Zenith Stromberg was a damn sight cheaper carburettor than the currently fitted Weber. Immediately, Steve Sanville and Graham Atkins were asked to make whatever alterations were necessary to accommodate the change. Elans fitted with twin Stromberg carburettors became available in November that year. This seemingly small modification involved the Lotus team in a considerable amount of testing, especially of those Elans destined for the States, since the engine had to pass stiff American regulations. Eventually, Elans fitted with suitably 'clean' engines began to be exported, although the safety laws involving side intrusion regulations finally killed off Elan sales in the States. In spite of development work, from 1970 onwards Elans were again fitted with Weber.

'I was made an offer by Colin Chapman at the 1968 Motor Show to join Lotus' recalled Tony Rudd, 'but at the time I'd agreed with Sir Alfred Owen at BRM to stay on. It soon became clear to me, though, that as things were going at BRM, I would have to make a move. So, on the way to the Zandvoort GP I asked Mr Chapman if the offer was still open, to which he replied, "Come and see me." I joined Lotus on 3 September, 1969.'

Colin and Tony had been quite good friends since 1957 and Chapman later commissioned BRM to undertake a design study for a new Elan engine. BRM produced some paper design studies for a 2-litre 120-degree V6 based on the twin-cam combustion chamber and valve shape. Chapman was impressed with the proposal. He said it did everything he wanted but he thought it was too wide to fit between the front wheels of an Elan on full lock. The project was killed there and then.

Chapman's edict to Rudd was to productionise the new Lotus Type 907 2-litre engine. He was to be given a six-month settling in period whereupon, if all was well, Rudd would become Engineering Director. Meanwhile, there was the small problem of a large surplus of unsold Elans on the test track, a sight Chapman could not miss when he looked out of his office window!

'I hadn't been with the company long when the phone went. You always knew when it was Chunky (Mr Chapman's nickname) because it seemed to have an ominous ring, almost jumping off the table' explained Tony.

An S4 coupe and drophead. Among the changes on this version were the flared wheelarches and larger tyres, twin pipe exhaust, collapsible steering column and rocker switches on the facia.

'Lotus Engineering were making more Elans than were being sold. I was Engineering Director, what was I going to do about it?'

Rudd suggested to Chapman that the solution was an honest twenty per cent or thereabouts increase in power (103bhp to 128bhp). However, since Rudd had been involved with the BRM-developed Elan racing engines he already had experience. The compression ratio was raised, the ports opened out to accommodate bigger inlet valves, high lift camshafts fitted to take advantage of the cylinder head modifications and the jets and chokes altered in the Webers. A quick 'lunch run' in the prototype Big Valve Elan proved to Chapman that when using all the power in all gears at all times, it was 'bloody good'. Rudd also modified the differential carrier and Rotaflex couplings to take the extra power and torque. Meanwhile, the marketing and styling teams took advantage of the chance for publicity. The cam covers were given a black crackle finish while the body paintwork was two-tone gold leaf, the car being known as the Elan Sprint. However, the most ingenious of all the changes made to the latest version of the Elan had no relation to the engine at all!

'As time went on, the GRP manufacturing process was being further refined and with the introduction of the Elan Sprint we took the opportunity to introduce the combined laminating and painting idea' recalled Albert Adams, 'so that the lower half of the Elan Sprint bodies emerged from the mould ready painted.'

Although the Big Valve Sprint in both drophead and coupe forms was launched at the 1970 London Show, deliveries did not begin until some way into the following year. 'As for the Elans we had in stock at Hethel, we systematically changed out the cylinder heads one by one, modifying them as we went, painting the bottoms of the doors gold,' explained Tony. The very last few Elan Sprints were fitted with five-speed gearboxes before production stopped in mid-1973. Lotus continued to make the twin-cam engine until March 1975 (fitted to the Lotus Europa) when, unceremoniously it was finally dropped. Another, bigger all-Lotus-made engine was waiting in the wings. By this time, of course, Ford had introduced their new 2-litre 'Pinto'-engined range of cars, maintaining manufacture of the Lotus-type cylinder blocks simply for Lotus's own consumption. (Lotus supplied Ford with engines for use in the Escort twin cam.)

Over its ten-year lifespan, model development on the Elan was always done hurriedly in the face of falling sales. The final straw was the increasingly stringent US safety laws. The Elan, however, had become a legend in its own lifetime, with a fanatical following few other sports cars could match.

3 The Family Elan

LOTUS FLOURISHES

From the nail-biting period of the early 1960s when Lotus had reached the point of no return after stopping Elite production, but with some time to go before the Elan would hit the showrooms, 1963, 1964 and 1965 were boom years for the Cheshunt-based company. Elan sales were spiralling and the Lotus Cortina, too, was creating great interest both on and off the competition circuits. Things in the Lotus garden were certainly blooming. As Fred Bushell said:

'The number of people who have devoted a large part of their working lives to Lotus is incredible. Working for Lotus was rather like being on drugs, we were so buoyed up by a sense of achievement. I have always felt that the chance decision to call the company "Lotus" rather than, say, "Chapman Motors"

was one reason behind the company's success because we could all feel part of it. Most people felt they were working for Lotus, not Colin Chapman.'

Ron Hickman agrees that Chapman was somehow able to fire people with such enthusiasm that it affected everyone on the team.

'We all learnt at five times the rate that we would have done anywhere else,' explained Hickman, recalling the period when they were developing the Elan. 'There was a lot of thinking done when developing a particular component, perhaps just one prototype of it made and then we'd go into production. We had a lot of freedom. Just remember, the design, development and productionising of the Elan took only £27,000 — less than the cost of productionising a bumper bar in a large company!'

Putting things into perspective, when the Elite was launched, Chapman was twenty-nine years old. His first Grand Prix win was three years later. Moreover, such was Ford's respect for his talent and that of his company that in the summer of 1962 a delegation arrived from Detroit to discuss the Ford GT40 programme with Chapman. History has recorded that the GT40 Project Manager, Roy Lunn, was concerned that Chapman would steal his thunder. He had a right to be worried! Later, Sir William Lyons talked to Chapman, too, concerning a possible deal over the company. All the while, Kirwan-Taylor and Fred Bushell were whispering words of wisdom with regard to not losing control of the Lotus operation.

The most powerful version of Lotus's tohc engine can be identified by the 'Big Valve' cam cover.

An Elan Plus 2S 130/5.

While the Elan was now firmly establishing a growing band of enthusiastic followers, in concept at least it had moved a considerable way from the basic Lotus Seven replacement Chapman had had in mind during the late 1950s. Although the Ford-based tohc power unit was much cheaper than the low volume Coventry–Climax engine used in the Elite, Elan manufacturing costs dictated that the retail price be pegged some way above what could reasonably be asked for a latter-day Seven.

DEVELOPING THE +2

Surprisingly, despite the urge to move his company (and its products) away from the image of being a kit car manufacturer, Chapman still gave great thought to a small, basic car; a cross, almost, between a beach buggy and a true sports car. He also gave some consideration to a multi-purpose design, the basis of which would have a 2+2 interior and be offered in either removable hard-top form, fixed hard-top form or estate variants.

'I left the company about the time of the early styling proposals for the Lotus Seven and the Elan' recalled John Frayling recently. 'The styling for the Elan +2 was carried out by Ron Hickman and his team. Colin's brief was that the car should have the front of the Elan and the rear of the Elite. I'd left to set up on my own, although around the time the +2 was being conceived Peter Kirwan-Taylor and I did a lot of styling for Lotus including the 23 and the Formula Junior. Later, if Colin wanted me to make a subtle change to something he'd call me in to do it.'

Tests on the Elan's backbone chassis had proved it to be extremely rigid and more than capable of forming the foundation for a larger design. Extra inches were added to the Elan's chassis to create greater length in the wheelbase which in turn would provide the room necessary for the +2 rear seats.

Work on the family man's Elan began in 1964 with a first cut styling proposal displayed to a gathering of people from the

An Elan +2 body-shell showing the seam between the top and bottom sections.

motor press in 1965 in order to gauge reaction and listen to criticisms. By adding several inches to the chassis, the line of the front wing and doors was extended to give the car a sleeker appearance, while the frontal area was cleaned up and lengthened slightly, all of which improved its general shape over the earlier, stubbier Elan. However, while opinion was generally favourable, many thought the styling too narrow for its length. Chapman, however, was less than happy with the whole front end and said that it should follow more the pattern of the Rover–BRM Le Mans project. He also instructed that the track should be wider. Several attempts were made to satisfy him before a total of 7in (17.8cm) had been added and he was happy with the result. The final chassis dimension for the +2 had grown by some 12in (30.5cm) in the wheelbase and 7in (17.8cm) in the track. This, in turn, made it possible to increase the overall length of the +2 by a considerable 23in (58.4cm) and an extra 10in (25.4cm) in the overall width.

As for the car's production engineering, at last the design team at Lotus were learning the skills the specialist boys had known for many years: that the cheapest way to build low-volume cars was to buy in as many parts as possible from large manufacturers.

'One of the first decisions we made over the +2 was that we wanted to use all the brightwork from the front· of the Ford Capri, including the steel pressing and the glass' added Albert Adams. 'We made the door and windscreen apertures so that we could buy in the complete package from Ford. I also remember that we were having difficulties over styling the rear end of the +2. One evening I was driving home from work, following an Alfa Romeo Guillia. I was watching his brake lights coming on and thinking how the design of the light cluster would be so right for our new car. The following morning I suggested we look at these lights and in the event we designed the

+2 specifically to accept the Alfa Romeo rear light set-up, recessing the boot wall to take them. However, we could only buy these lights in large quantities so we redesigned the Elan and the Europa (the mid-engined car) so that they, too, could utilise the same light cluster.'

Other parts for the +2 from volume production models included the front bumper from the Ford Anglia saloon and a manufactured rear bumper made from a Wolseley Hornet bumper cut in half with an extra section added in the centre.

In its final shape, the new +2 was, indeed, a handsome-looking car. Aerodynamically, it was also a very efficient car for the additional length made a cleaner profile for better wind flow while the extra width (with its less bulbous lines) produced less air turbulence. The result was an outstandingly low coefficient of drag rating of 0.3. (Compare this with, say, a Porsche of the same period which was rated at 0.36.) Externally, the Elan +2 had a more mature shape than the tiny Elan sports, with an elegance and purity of line which few other stylists could match during the mid-1960s. Indeed, it still stands the test of time magnificently. There is a balance about the +2's proportions which makes focusing on the car's dimensions a difficult task. It is, in fact, much smaller than most photographs would suggest.

Not surprisingly, the +2· is also proportionally that much heavier than its twoseater sister, the extra size adding a full 3cwt (152.4kg) to the Elan's lithe 14cwt (711.2kg). But few could quibble over the benefits created by the larger body for as well as the 'proper' rear seats, the added 10in (25.4cm) to the car's width overcame the slightly cramped feeling some owners felt in the Elan. Part of that additional 3cwt (152.4kg) could be attributed to enthusiastic use of sound deadening in an effort to reduce noise – all part of the planned move up-market to the exclusive Grand Touring Class!

The +2's extra 7½in (19.05cm) width over the Elan contributed to the car's outstanding cornering.

Naturally, braking and suspension were altered as part of the +2 package. The front disc brakes were now 10in (25.4cm) with servo assistance, while spring and damper settings were altered to accept the greater weight, together with 165 × 13in tyres. Roadholding on the +2 was very much a match for the smaller Elan because weight distribution had been set almost identically at 48/52 per cent front to back, while cornering had to be considered marginally improved in view of the wider track.

Under the bonnet, Lotus overcame the slight weight penalty by installing the Special Equipment engine as fitted to the Lotus Cortina (the version built at Dagenham) which boasted new piston crowns for better combustion, bigger exhaust valves and new jets and chokes in the twin Weber carburettors. Power was rated at 118bhp (net), sufficient to give a true top speed of 125mph (201.2kph) and a 0–60mph (0–96.5kph) time of 8.2sec. A 3.7 final drive helped marginally to counterbalance the extra weight and the car's impressive aerodynamics played a vital role in producing its excellent performance.

'While the move from Cheshunt to Hethel was to herald a whole new chapter in the company's history,' said Albert Adams, 'I clearly recall that the change of location also earmarked the first drive of the prototype Elan +2, which was followed by an anxious development engineer in an Elan who was detailed to "pick anything up which happened to fall off".' 'I was never all that impressed by the Elan,' added Tony Rudd candidly, 'although I thought the +2 was a very handsome car.'

The +2 was introduced in June 1967 in fixed hard-top form only. Since the early days of the Elan, Lotus had learned quickly how to trim and finish interiors and the +2's cabin looked most luxurious with its comfortable, hip-hugging front seats and wood-veneered dashboard. Through-flow ventilation was there to help soothe the brows of driver and passengers. However, for tall people, room in

The frontal appearance of the Elan Plus 2 was influenced by the Rover – BRM Le Mans project sports racing car of the period (right).

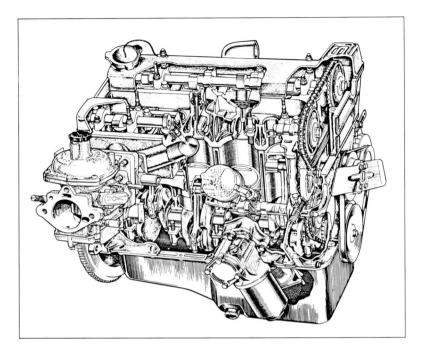

Engine cutaway.

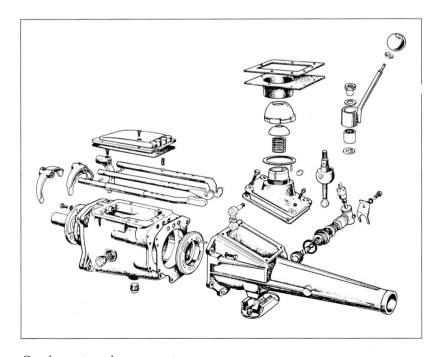

Gearbox external components.

the rear was limited; this space was really intended for young children. Of course, all this opulence came at a substantial price. At £1,923 the +2 was a huge £797 more than the MGB GT.

'We were always trying to run before we could walk at Lotus' recalled Ron Hickman regretfully. 'The finances just weren't there and I began to realise that the harder I pushed myself, the quicker I was heading for an early grave. By 1967 my contract had already run out, although Colin knew that he needed certain key people when he moved to Hethel. But I was tired and bored so I decided to leave.'

At a stroke, Lotus lost a very talented and capable project engineer. ('Unlike myself, Hickman was a very thorough designer,' said John Frayling.) Indeed, it is rumoured that of three key men who left Lotus – Graham Warner, Mike Costin and Ron Hickman – Chapman never really forgave any of them. 'Chapman was a very good captain but a very poor navigator,' said Hickman.

SUCCESS AT LAST

If Colin Chapman allowed himself the luxury to look back on his achievements and those of

The Elan +2 production line in 1968.

LOTUS +2 AND PLUS 2S

Approximately 1,600 +2s were built between June 1967 and December 1969; approximately 3,000 Plus 2Ss were built between March 1969 and December 1974; chassis numbers were from 50/0001, 7001, 7101, 7201, 7301 and 7401.

Engine
As for Special Equipment and Sprint Elan models.

Chassis
Weight (on road)   1,848−1,932lb (838.3−876.4kg)
Wheelbase   8ft (2.44m)
Front track   4ft 6in (1.37m)
Rear track   4ft 7in (1.4m)
Length   14ft (4.27m)
Width   5ft 3.5in (1.61m)
Height   3ft 11in (1.19m)
Turning circle   34ft (10.36m)
Suspension   As Elan
Gearbox
Four-speed − overall ratios with 3.77 rear axle:
  1st gear   3.77
  2nd gear   5.27
  3rd gear   7.57
  4th gear   11.20
  reverse   12.53
Optional five-speed on later models − overall ratios with 3.77 rear axle:
  1st gear   3.28
  2nd gear   3.77
  3rd gear   5.16
  4th gear   7.54
  5th gear   12.06
  reverse   13.08
Steering   rack and pinion
Wheels and tyres   165−13

the company when he laid the foundation stone at Hethel he should have been very pleased with his track record. The stone was engraved with the simple words: 'Layed on the 17th July 1966 by Colin Chapman, Founder'. In less than twenty years he had established a world renowned organisation with himself at its helm. On the racing side, Jim Clark had won two Formula 1 World Championships driving Lotus cars in 1963 and 1965, while on the domestic sports car market he had successfully achieved his goal of moving his products up-market and away from the kit car 'specials' image to that of the elegant grand tourer for the upwardly mobile family man whose car described his personality. The launch of the +2 had further strengthened this plan by converting a whole new sector of the buying public into Lotus enthusiasts.

Built on an ex-USAF bomber airfield, Lotus's new home at Hethel had some 151,000sq ft (14,030sq m) of assembly and stores area based in a single-storey block plus a further 26,000sq ft (2,400sq m) of open-plan office space. A far cry from the tiny lock-up

The sleek and elegant lines of the Elan Plus 2S 130 are enhanced by the use of 'pop-up' headlights.

garage behind Hazel's home in north London.

Initially, the +2 was available in kit form as well as fully assembled, although the number of customers who were prepared to build their own cars began to dwindle. This was, of course, exactly what Colin was encouraging. Shortly after the +2's introduction several changes were made to the design of the twin-cam engine in an effort to make it more robust and reliable; the main bearing caps were modified and the pistons changed to a higher grade. A team of mainly ex-RAF fitters, chosen for their high quality of workmanship, were employed on engine assembly. Machining facilities were set up so that the sand castings from William Mills could be prepared and the engines assembled in-house. Indeed, compared with the traumas of the day-to-day dealings with JAP and Norton Villiers (who were responsible for initial engine assembly), Lotus were able to establish a highly efficient production line. In eight years, Hethel built 25,500 engines

The Elan Plus 2S 130 on display at the London Motor Show.

compared to 7,100 in the first four years of the engine's life when the units were assembled by sub-contract. Improved casting quality and higher standards of engine assembly ensured a significant improvement in reliability. Again, all part of the Lotus master plan to move its cars and image into the executive sports car market.

Like the Elan, the specification of the +2's engine was changed by the move from Weber to Stromberg carburettors in an effort to reduce costs and make the engine compatible with the American emission laws. Graham Atkins had proved that he could make the twin-cam engine every bit as powerful as the earlier Weberised version, although a great deal of development work had to be done by both Lotus and Zenith for what would only be a little over twelve months of US sales. An uneven engine beat on tick over and carburettor icing were two shortfalls, although the Stromberg returned better fuel economy and smoother performance.

ELAN PLUS 2S

Meanwhile, the +2 had been passed for sale in the US, its metal inserts in the sills giving it a higher side intrusion resistance. In March 1969 the Plus 2S was introduced. It was the first Lotus road car which was not available in kit form and retained the Weber carburettors. For the American market the +2 was retained in production with the intention of introducing a 'clean' version of the Plus 2S engine for the States later. Inside, the dashboard was improved by the addition of more comprehensive instrumentation with a lot of extras, such as fog lights, fitted as standard. GKN spent some time perfecting a special design of alloy wheel and these were fitted as part of the Plus 2S's specification, while the design of the driveshaft doughnut couplings was modified to improve their strength. In December 1969 the +2 was dropped. By this time, demand for the 'S' version was

The Elan Plus 2's commendable top speed owed much to its sleek body shape.

The Plus 2S 130/5 was fitted with a five-speed gearbox which gave the car a delightful high-speed cruising ability.

The impressive styling of the Elan Plus 2S 130/5 makes it an exceptional car.

Access to the brake servo, wiper motor and exhaust manifold is straightforward.

*The wiring behind the full-width veneer dashboard is revealed.
The dashboard and comprehensive instrumentation contributed
to the Elan +2's luxurious interior.*

*Hidden beneath the twin Weber carburettors, the distributor
and fuel pump are difficult to get at.*

The luxurious interior of the Plus 2S 130/5.

outstripping the earlier model, thereby confirming Chapman's theory that anyone thinking of buying a car in the +2 category could probably afford the extra for the better equipped version.

As we have seen with the Elan, Tony Rudd developed the Big Valve engine as a way to inject renewed life into the sales figures. Rudd's solution was to work the cylinder heads so that 1.6in (4.1cm) inlet valves could be used in place of the existing 1.32in (3.4cm) ones, and machine the faces to raise the compression ratio to 10.3:1. In addition to this, the camshafts were changed to 'D' type versions and the Stromberg carburettors

replaced by cheaper twin DHLA40 Dellortos. This gave a reputed output of 126bhp at 5,500rpm when measured at the prop shaft (compared to 101bhp at 6,250rpm of the S/Es unit when tested at the same point). For the States, however, initial exports had to rely on the less powerful small valve engine until the Stromberg carburettors could be made to give the same performance. On the home market, the cost price of Weber carburettors began to fall as competition from the cheaper Dellortos began to bite and Webers were, once again, adopted as part of the European specification.

Announced in October 1970, the latest

version of the 2+2 Elan was known as the Plus 2S 130 (with just a little public relations licence). However, impatient customers had to wait until February 1971 before deliveries began.

'At the time, Lotus Sales were ordering more cars from Lotus Engineering than were actually being sold,' recalled Tony Rudd, 'which resulted in a large quantity of unsold cars on our test track. I'd told Colin that we needed a genuine increase of around 25bhp to rejuvenate sales. To solve the problem of the cars lined up outside we changed over the cylinder heads, one at a time, and sprayed the roofs of the Plus 2Ss silver.' (On later cars the silver paintwork on the roof formed part of the moulding process, an ingenious idea which was developed on more contemporary Lotus models.)

To cope with the additional power, the driveshaft splines were reduced in length and additional sections were let into the chassis around the differential mounting to accommodate the extra torque being transmitted. The driveshaft doughnuts were increased in strength and, as a final thought, the pop-up headlight operation was altered so that – as a safety measure – the vacuum action was used to keep them in their closed position.

The final stage in the Plus 2's development programme involved the addition of a five-speed gearbox. With the introduction of the front-wheel-drive five-door Austin Maxi, Chapman could see a use for the five-speed gear cluster since it gave a lower first gear and higher fifth gear than the current Ford box. A special gearbox casing was designed to take the Maxi cogs and, after initial difficulties with a stiff movement, this box became available, the car being known as the Plus 2S 130/5. Its beauty was that it endowed the larger Elan with a more relaxed character since maximum speed could be reached with 1,400revs less than in the four-speed car.

'Early Elan Plus 2s did give problems because it was a fairly sophisticated car' Tony Rudd recalled candidly. 'The wiring loom, for example, was pretty complex because of all the gadgets, each of which needed an earth return because the body was made from GRP. Then we employed an ex-Rolls-Royce apprentice called Martin Drury and he did a first class job improving quality.'

Bill Brown, who was a member of the manufacturing team, recalled that although it is true that the Elan Plus 2 (and the smaller Elan) did become more complex as time went on, assembly became easier as development was done to aid the build process.

As for Plus 2 estates and convertibles, Albert Adams is adamant that these non-Lotus developed conversions were very much against the Chapman philosophy:

'You have to understand the nature of the man' he said. 'He was very much the purist in his approach to styling. He didn't like to see his designs messed about or bits added on. He developed the cars he wanted to manufacture. The design of the Plus 2's body structure did not lend itself to having the roof cut away. The roof and the windscreen were intended to be an integral unit to take the stresses imposed by road irregularities.'

Without hesitation, everyone involved with Lotus during the period when the Elan and the Elan Plus 2 were being developed look back with strong feelings, both for the work and for Chapman.

'Although Colin could be a hard taskmaster,' recalled Tony Rudd, 'he could also be very kind. When I burst a blood vessel in my eye, he had Fred Bushell arrange for tickets to fly my wife and I on holiday and we were able to stay on for extra time when he instructed Fred to mail through my bonus.'

'I remember I was developing a new moulding process and felt that I was pushing an emotional stone up a hill' said Albert Adams recalling a poignant moment in his relationship with Chapman. 'Colin gave me a brand new Plus 2 and a further push up the hill.'

'We never regarded it as work' admitted Ron Hickman who, like John Frayling, contributed so much during the Elan days. 'It was the most exciting time of my life. Colin had great charm and I was just glad to have been part of it.'

'Colin was one of the few captains of industry who actually had the qualifications to do the job' said John Frayling whose time with Lotus and Chapman continued until Colin died in 1982. 'He had tremendous charm and I admired him for his courage. He used his team like tools.'

4 Elan on the Move

As history has already recorded, at the time of the Elan's launch to the public in 1962, there was precious little in the way of finance to support the company and, hardly surprisingly, little thought had been given to promoting the new car: all efforts being concentrated on the simple matter of keeping Lotus afloat! Worse (if that was possible), as Graham Arnold learned when he moved from a senior marketing job with Ford to join Lotus in May 1963 to handle promotion, one of the company's salesmen had only recently left having created nothing more than a fictitious list of Elan sales and clutching the commission cheque as he did so.

Perhaps the lack of a composite sales and marketing strategy prior to Arnold's arrival can be partly attributed to Chapman's genuine dislike of customers for his cars (remember how Fred Bushell had to take over handling sales of the Elite in the very early days at Tottenham). Indeed, it seems that (according to Arnold) while in theory there had been much feverish activity over creating sales interest in the Elan, in truth few had actually put down hard cash and there was little in the way of confirmed orders.

Arnold immediately set about organising a mail-shot programme and sent out a considerable number of letters to people from many walks of life inviting them to come and try the little Elan for size at its Motor Show début in London. The situation was not without a degree of irony for many who received these invitations mistook them for a free entry to the Show! Nevertheless, the idea worked and a steady stream of professional people with bowler hats and umbrellas could be seen easing themselves into Chapman's

latest model and probably many were surprised by the amount of space there was, once inside.

ROAD TESTS

Elan Series 1

Somewhat curiously, while production of the Series 1 Elan struggled into life during the early part of 1963 (at that time Lotus were still making the Elite) *Autocar* — one of Britain's leading motoring magazines — did not manage to get a car for a full road test until mid-1964, shortly before the release of the Series 2. Yet for all this delay, the motor noters from *Autocar* were highly delighted with their first test of the marque saying that 'Without doubt the Elan is a sports car — thorough-bred because it owes its characteristics almost entirely to Lotus racing experience'. In the light of its curious styling (most people — some still do — felt that the Elan's looks were no match for its predecessor, the Elite), it was quite clearly the Elan's performance and roadholding which endeared itself to *Autocar*'s staff. They were encouraged to comment that 'In its superior fits and finish alone it shows an important advance over the Elite'. Even this has to be relative since this model Elan still had push up windows and a rather crude, confused wood-veneer dashboard. That said, there were some who were less than happy about certain aspects and said 'There were mixed feelings about the appearance of the instrument panel, some saying that the layout is bitty and the woodwork amateurish'. When it came to the seats, however, it

was a different story for '. . . everyone on our
staff approved the shape and comfort of the
bucket seats'.

When it came to reviewing the car's
handling *Autocar* writers talked of 'almost
uncanny cornering power' and 'road adhesion that was well above average' – to say
nothing of the 'quick light steering'. And, if
this was not enough, when it came to
describing how the little car went they said
'The combination of a lusty engine, quick
gearbox and light car can give an exhilarating performance as may be seen from
the measured performance figures'.

As for the power unit, the feature was
equally complimentary, saying: 'As one
would expect, the car owes a good deal of its
attraction to the twin-cam Ford – Lotus
engine, now of 1,558cc capacity' and that
'This is remarkably tractable, docile at slow
speeds, quiet and with the pull of a lion from
2,000 to 6,500rpm in top gear'. Finally, they
said 'To those with misgivings about the
durability, and thus the value for money, of
the Lotus Elan, we can only say at this stage
that the car seems much stronger and better
made than some of its predecessors . . .'
'Anyone to whom the Elan is likely to appeal
should try to arrange a trial run because this
is very much a driver's car'.

So much then for *Autocar*'s comments on
the Series 1 Elan. Late though it was, the
words do give a clear idea of how highly the
car was rated for its sheer driveability. It
was, indeed, a car which the enthusiast could
rave over, despite its shortfalls. But, with the
quiet demise of the Elite, Lotus no longer had
a fixed hard-top to offer the customer who did
not revel in wind-in-the-hair motoring. That
was until the launch of the Lotus Elan coupe
the following year.

Comparison: Elite, Elan Coupe and Elan Roadster

Somehow, perhaps because it was a fixed
hard-top and therefore did not suffer the

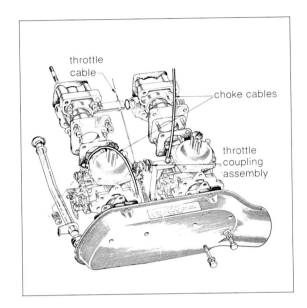

*Air box and carburretor assembly
(Zenith Stromberg).*

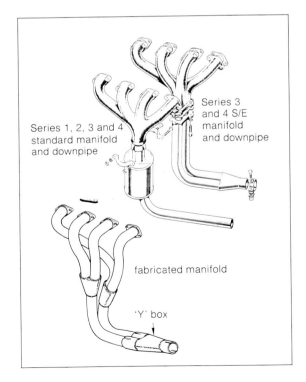

Exhaust manifolds and downpipes.

LOTUS ELITE (S/E) – Performance at a Glance

Speeds in the gears
1st	40mph	(64.37kph)
2nd	68mph	(109.43kph)
3rd	99mph	(159.32kph)
4th	115mph	(185.07kph)

Acceleration
0–30 (0–48.23)	4.3sec
0–40 (0–64.37)	6.1sec
0–50 (0–80.47)	8.2sec
0–60 (0–96.56)	11.3sec
0–70 (0–112.65)	14.5sec
0–80 (0–128.74)	18.4sec

Fuel consumption   34.2 mpg (55.04 kpg) overall

Figures courtesy of *Car* Giant Road Test, January 1966

LOTUS ELAN – Performance at a Glance

		Series 1 Roadster	Series 2 Coupe	Sprint Roadster
Speeds in the gears	1st	46mph (74.03kph)	45mph (72.42kph)	41mph (65.98kph)
	2nd	70mph (112.65kph)	70mph (112.65kph)	58mph (112.65kph)
	3rd	92mph (148.06kph)	92mph (148.06kph)	86.5mph (139.2kph)
	4th	114mph (183.46kph)	110mph (177.02kph)	121mph (194.73kph)
Acceleration	0–30 (0– 48.23)	3.3sec	3.4sec	2.5sec
	0–40 (0– 64.37)	4.7sec	4.4sec	3.6sec
	0–50 (0– 80.47)	6.6sec	5.5sec	5.4sec
	0–60 (0– 96.56)	8.7sec	7.6sec	6.7sec
	0–70 (0–112.65)	11.5sec	10.4sec	9.4sec
	0–80 (0–128.74)	15.1sec	12.1sec	12.0sec
Fuel consumption		27.9mpg (44.9kpg) overall	24.6mpg (39.6kpg)	22.2mpg (35.73kpg)

Figures courtesy of *Autocar*, August 1964; *Car*, January 1966; *Motor*, March 1971

irregular lines of the open car, the coupe managed to look much sleeker. Ostensibly, the only change was the deeper windscreen, though the fixed roof with its gracefully sloping rear window gave the car an elegance the open car clearly lacked. In one of *Car* magazine's large multi-test features (for which it has become so popular over the years), Graham 'Mr Fix-it' Arnold had managed to supply not only a fixed hard-top *and* a soft-top Elan but had also unearthed the original road test Elite which Lotus had salted away for posterity. In January 1966 *Car* had the unique opportunity to try all three cars together and make their judgements.

From the early days, magazine road testers the world over always rated the Elan's roadholding very highly — yet it was achieved at no reduction in ride comfort.

An Elan Sprint with its hood erected. *Motor* complained that putting up the hood was, 'fiddly' although once there it proved to be, 'draft-free'.

An Elan Sprint with non-standard alloy wheels and flared wheelarches. 'Hood down,' said Motor *'the Elan Sprint epitomises sports car motoring.'*

With the three cars lined up side-by-side, the team from *Car* had the ideal opportunity to compare styles. 'Visually,' they said 'all our staff were unanimous in declaring the Elite the best-looking of the three cars we assessed. The Elan coupe came next and the roadster last.' However, *Car* did qualify their statement by admitting that this was partly due to the different engine installation which allowed for a lower bonnet line and the fixed side windows which meant that the curvature of the doors could be made more pronounced. Even so, they were forced to say that 'Despite obvious stylistic similarities, particularly at the back and around the bonnet opening, it [the Elan] seems to lack the sheer inspiration that gives the Elite its beauty.'

Not surprisingly, this opportunity to compare like with like showed up some interesting features: while the boot space on the Elan coupe was smaller through having to accommodate the battery, on the Elan roadster and the Elite the boot space was found to be very similar. Moreover, while the windows on the open car were manually operated there seemed to be little difference between the benefits of the completely open or completely shut attitude of the Elite and the infuriatingly slow electric window lifts of the coupe. However, perhaps what was even more surprising – in view of the fact that both the Elite and the Elan were products of a racing-orientated company who, one would assume, should have known better – neither the Elite nor the Elan dashboard arrangements came in for any degree of praise. The Elite's switches were described as 'confusing' and 'very stiff to operate', while the Elan's were said to have had 'a distinct Standard – Triumph look about it'. Could it be that racing drivers get what they are given when it comes to the dashboard layout and controls whereas customers for road cars can afford to be more choosy?

Significantly, an interesting comment which emerged when comparing the two engine installations described the Elite as being a much easier unit to work on than the Elan's, saying that access to the distributor was especially awkward. As for the Weber carburettors, they were considered to be 'beyond the scope of all but a dozen or so skilled men in this country'. Hmmm...

Performance-wise, the Elite turned out to be the fastest of the trio – as the performance tables show – but it was by far the noisiest, too, and there were severe reservations about the occupants actually being able to withstand the din of travelling at 120mph (193.1kph) for very long, '... at that speed the noise level becomes altogether too high and there are additional long-term problems such as mild vibration'. As for the open Elan, that too was hardly quiet and suffered from the usual drawbacks associated with sports cars. With the hood down there was buffeting from wind entering the cabin, while with the hood up there was much flapping and slapping. 'Mechanical noises become apparent, the gear lever vibration grows worse, with the hood up there is a lot of unpleasant wind noise and drumming and with it down you get sharply buffeted by the backdraught.' Again, the accolades went to the coupe. The fixed hard-top and Lotus's obvious attention to extra sound deadening had paid dividends and *Car* said that 'it was outstandingly quiet right up to its maximum speed'.

As one might expect of cars with their background, the steering and braking – even on the older Elite – were reckoned to be pretty impressive. It was in the suspension department, though, where the greatest differences were noticed since the younger Elan now benefited from Mr Chapman's theories on softly sprung sports cars. 'It is the first car in its class to equate a really soft ride (this is not a relative term) with sporting handling, and as such it deserves applause. We can truly say that in most situations the blend works well.' With their different suspension set-ups, the Elite and the Elan proved to have substantially contrasting roadholding manners. The Elite displayed large amounts of understeer right up to the limit, at which point the inside front wheel was very firmly lifted off the ground, while the Elan produced far greater roll but maintained its chosen line. *Car* called the Elite's handling 'classical' while the Elan was considered to have the greater compromise between soft springing and impressive cornering abilities.

Elan +2

By September 1967 *Motor* had got their hands on an Elan +2 and − if the opening paragraph is any measure of the car's capabilities − the team were clearly impressed for they began by saying 'This report is something of a landmark in the history of *Motor* road tests'. By any stretch of the imagination, any test which opens with words such as these must be full of superlatives. And so it turned out to be in almost

all respects. 'Let's be specific' they continued. 'The uncanny cornering powers of this remarkable machine equal or exceed those of any other production car we have driven.' Gripping words but it was, after all, a Lotus they were talking about.

Equally impressive was the car's performance. Chapman's 'Let's stick a tohc head on a cooking Ford block' was proving to be outstandingly successful and certainly endowed the bigger Elan with stirring performance. 'Greater performance can be bought elsewhere,' continued *Motor*, 'but according to our records no other four-seater is capable of reaching 60mph (96.5kph) in only 8.2 sec or a maximum speed of 125mph (201.2kph) on a mere 1,600cc.' In fact, someone at Hethel had forgotten to fit the ignition cut-out and the road test car achieved a best one-way speed of 125mph (201.2kph) well over the maker's 6,500rpm limit.

Such performance was the result of the sleekly styled body. Lotus even claimed that the drag coefficient was the lowest yet

A smiling Colin Chapman outside his north London home with an Elan and an Elan +2.

*The neat rear treatment seen here on this Elan S4 Drophead.
Motor commented that the single tail-pipe exhaust was much
quieter than the earlier twin-pipe version.*

*Surprisingly, despite its racing heritage the arrangement of the
Elan's dashboard switches was never rated that highly by motor
noters.*

A 1970 Elan S4 drophead. Road & Track *magazine called the Elan, 'a gutty little car, highly refined in some ways and crude in others', when they tested an S4 S/E in January 1969.*

achieved on a production car. But the body was not only streamlined, it was also extremely attractive. 'Not many people are going to contradict us, either, if we suggest that this is one of the finest looking cars to be designed in Britain today,' said *Motor*.

As in the case of the Elan coupe, the +2's fixed hard-top gave it an unfussy elegance of line that the soft-top models could never hope to achieve. Moreover, its broad sloping snout was a distinct improvement over the small Elan. An immediate benefit of the wide dimensions of the Elan +2 is the extra elbow room between driver and passenger, the larger Lotus taking on a 'big car' feel. This

feeling is enhanced by the additional space in the rear which is sufficient (just) to accommodate two occasional seats. However, the amount of leg room really limits their use to small children; to create sufficient leg room for an adult, the front seat has to be pushed a long way forward. Even so, the rear seat passenger's head will almost certainly be touching the roof. 'Nevertheless,' said *Motor*, 'for short journeys, the accommodation here is tolerable for adults'.

Another important aspect of a car such as the +2 — especially on long journeys — is heating and ventilation. The fresh air system in the +2 was so good that *Motor* declared it

LOTUS ELAN PLUS 2 – Performance at a Glance

	Elan +2	Elan Plus 2 S/E	Elan Plus 2S 130
Speeds in the gears	1st 39mph (62.76kph)	40mph (64.37kph)	41mph (65.98kph)
	2nd 58mph (93.34kph)	60mph (80.47kph)	60mph (80.47kph)
	3rd 82mph (131.96kph)	86mph (138.4kph)	87mph (140.01kph)
	4th 114mph (201.16kph)	118mph (189.9kph)	121mph (194.73kph)
Acceleration	0–30 (0–48.23) 3.3sec	3.5sec	2.9sec
	0–40 (0–64.37) 4.5sec	4.9sec	4.1sec
	0–50 (0–80.47) 6.2sec	6.8sec	5.6sec
	0–60 (0–96.56) 8.2sec	8.9sec	7.4sec
	0–70 (0–112.65) 11.3sec	11.5sec	10.1sec
	0–80 (0–128.74) 14.4sec	15.0sec	12.7sec
Fuel consumption	24.5mpg (39.43kpg) overall	27.0mpg (43.45kpg)	23.0mpg (37.0 kpg)

Figures courtesy of *Motor*, September 1967; *Autocar*, March 1968; *Autocar*, February 1971

to be 'excellent', although there was one criticism which forced them to point out that 'The heater is very powerful but stiff horizontal levers on our car made it difficult to control'.

Clearly, Lotus had learned much in the short time between the launch of the Elan and the +2. Gone was the horrid unprofessional plywood facia of the first Elan roadster. In its place was a polished veneered panel with a comprehensive array of instruments, as befitting a car such as this. 'Both inside and out, the finish is very good' said *Motor*. Lotus had obviously spent some effort, too, ensuring that vibration levels entering the cabin were kept to a minimum for, 'With the windows up, the very smooth engine is fairly quiet, and very little noise penetrates the glass-fibre skin until the revs exceed 5,000rpm. Only with an open window can you detect that there is a sharp, crisp buzz of quite considerable volume coming from the exhaust, emphasising the efficiency of the body sound insulation'.

But all this work on designing a powerful, willing engine, a sumptuous interior and elegant exterior would be of no avail if the handling and roadholding did not give the driver a high degree of confidence. But this is an area – perhaps above all others – where the Chapman team really know their craft. 'Here we can only talk in superlatives' enthused *Motor*. 'The roadholding on the ordinary [ordinary?] Elan is remarkable enough but the bigger +2, with its much wider track and 165 × 13in tyres (on 5.5J rims) which plant an enormous amount of rubber on the road, is even better.'

Chapman's combination of soft spring rates and hardish damper settings – together with wide (for the period) wheels – produced cornering abilities which clearly had *Motor*'s noters reaching for their mental yardsticks, setting the Elan against other, more exotic machinery. They soon found that, without altering speed, the irrepressible Lotus would happily take corners which called for heavy braking beforehand and care in negotiating if taken in less capable cars. 'You cannot fail to be thrilled and enthralled by the novelty of this sort of cornering' they mused, and carried on to say, 'Invariably it is your nerve that gives way long before the impressive adhesion of the Dunlop SP41 tyres.'

Elan +2 S/E

Just six months after this glowing test (in March 1968) *Autocar* managed to lay their hands on a +2 (Special Equipment). The difference was marked. Was this a shining example of Lotus's quality control at its most inconsistent low? Who can tell, but while the *Autocar* team were equally enthralled with the Elan's 'superb roadholding' there were other areas which clearly did not come up to the standards set by the earlier test car. Or was it simply a case of a difference of opinion?

To begin with, the *Autocar* Elan was supplied with its ignition cut-out control firmly in place ensuring that the revs in top were limited to 6,500rpm equating to 118mph (189.9kph) in full flight − some way down on *Motor*'s claimed 125mph (201.2kph). However, this speed was reached 'easily and quickly both ways [on the test track] in diabolical conditions, and even though the car

was game for a good deal more we lifted-off at this compulsory rev limit'. Even the engine itself did not share the same sewing-machine-smooth qualities of the car tested in September. *Autocar* said of it 'It is a smooth willing unit, with lots of torque low down the rev range. Towards maximum revs it gets harsh without being rough, so there is no mistaking this is a four-cylinder engine' and that 'At high speed one can never forget that this is a small, highly-stressed engine revving hard.'

They also commented that the ride was set to give a harder response than on the smaller Elan, although they did admit that 'the spring and damper rates seem to be a good compromise'. Ironically, while the two cars shared the same gearbox (from the Cortina GT/Corsair 2000E) and gave rise to criticism from the *Motor* staff as being unsuitable for use in a sports car like the Elan +2, *Autocar* said that 'we found the gear ratios near-ideal, with close spacing'.

A Special Equipment Elan (S/E) which was fitted with knock-off wheels, servo assisted brakes and an uprated engine.

Taking the hood down starts with pulling the canvas away from the top of the screen . . .

. . . then holding it neatly to avoid creases in the perspex windows. Next . . .

. . . we can see the hood frame and the metal surround to the side windows. The hood frame itself . . .

. . . can be dismantled like this. Now we can see why Motor *were critical of the operation.*

Finally the hood can be stowed away neatly. It is important to use care in erecting and dismantling the hood to prevent the canvas from being damaged.

Surge in the transmission train was something which was, clearly, always going to be a bone of contention in both the Elan and the Elan +2 until the introduction of the stiffer doughnut Rotaflex couplings in the rear half shafts. 'It takes time and experience to overcome the inherent jerkiness' said *Autocar*. 'On the over-run, though, the "unwind" is at its worst, and there is not much the driver can do about that.'

Turning to the Elan's legendary handling they said: 'Everything is so delicately balanced that the first few miles are almost frightening.' Yet, like everyone who tested the Elan +2, the team revelled in its light, accurate steering. 'Behave clumsily,' they warned, 'and the car will respond accordingly.'

In terms of value-for-money, the £2,133 price tag for the factory-finished version of the +2 was a sharp reminder that the Lotus Elan was not a cheap car and the standard of finish led *Autocar* to mention that, 'we expected better quality control and attention to detail'. The problems? The same as many Lotus customers were complaining about: detail difficulties such as door locks failing, dashboard gauges not working and the wipers developing an intermittent fault. Worse, they said that 'The heater is rather ineffective, even with the two-speed fan set at "fast".' In many ways, it was because of these detail failings that Lotus's reputation took such a sharp knock, which was a pity in view of the glowing comments by automotive journalists regarding handling, ride and performance.

Elan Plus 2S 130

In early 1971 *Autocar* tested a Plus 2S 130, the big valve job developed by Tony Rudd. Among the many improvements which had been included were the beefed-up driveshaft couplings, the result being that – despite its high state of tune – the car was far easier to drive in town traffic. While peak power was rated at 6,500rpm (at which point the engine

The Elan Plus 2S received rave reviews from the press, getting high marks for roadholding, ride, performance and finish. It was also a very elegant car.

The smooth, elegant lines of the Plus 2S. Motor referred to the Elan Plus 2 as being, 'one of the finest looking cars to be designed and built in Britain'.

was reckoned to be producing 126bhp) this had not been achieved at the cost of low speed torque. *Autocar* found they could feed the clutch in at 1,200rpm and 'from then on the car can be trickled about at remarkably low speeds'. Using typical brutal road test techniques, the 130 was found to be able to accelerate to 60mph (96.5kph) in 7.4 sec – an identical time to that of the Jaguar E-Type 2+2.

By 1971 the choice of the 3.77 final drive ratio was beginning to be a distinct shortfall for this model of Elan and on this subject *Autocar* commented that 'On the whole the 3.77 final drive is a fair compromise, although it is hard to see why 3.55 is not offered as an alternative ... The ideal answer, of course, is a five-speed gearbox with an overdrive top, but there is no immediate prospect of this happening.' In fact, as we now know, that was just what Chapman was planning.

One aspect of the car's characteristics which had changed with the adoption of the big valve cylinder head was the fuel consumption. *Autocar*'s team got an overall consumption of only 23mpg (37kpg) – which admittedly included the acceleration and

The Plus 2 also had very adequate boot accommodation although the luggage had to be removed to get at the spare wheel.

The dashboard of an Elan Sprint. Surprisingly, some motoring enthusiasts felt the arrangement of the Elan's dashboard never came up to the design of the facia layout fitted to the earlier Elite.

By the introduction of the Elan Sprint in 1971 the pop-up headlight mechanism had been changed so that on full-throttle acceleration the lights did not drop down into the body.

Most testers agreed that the later treatment of the boot and rear light cluster was a great improvement.

The familiar Lotus badge with its founder's initials, 'ACBC' above.

For such a small car the Elan's boot was generous, Autocar referring to it as being, 'of convenient shape and reasonable size'.

maximum speed testing at MIRA — compared to 27mpg (43.5kpg) from the Special Equipment model they tested in March 1968.

The modifications to the driveshaft couplings, it seems, gave the driver extra confidence in the car's handling and, 'Once the driver has got used to the gentle approach needed [for steering] he can explore with confidence handling limits which are much higher than for most things on the road, even though standards have risen so much in the past three years.' A car which offers so much needs good brakes and *Autocar* had nothing but praise in this area, too. 'The brakes are incredibly reminiscent of those fitted to Alfas: very light in operation (thanks to a massive servo in the four disc system) and yet beautifully progressive, so that the driver can adjust his rate of stopping minutely.'

Interior comfort of the Plus 2S was clearly up to the standards set by previous models for front seat passengers. By the time this version of the Elan was introduced, the dashboard layout contained an impressive array of switches and dials — even if their individual location was confusing. The instrumentation included such items as an ambient temperature gauge which, surprisingly, took precedence over the oil pressure gauge which was sited way over on the passenger's side. The switch arrangement came in for comment, too: 'A jumble of identical switches makes life difficult for the driver, even though they are all within reach and all nicely labelled.'

The price of the car was another handicap, for the cost had risen from £2,113 in 1968 to

In their road test of the Elan Sprint drophead in 1971, Motor called this version of the Elan, 'Sports car par excellence' claiming with the introduction of the Sprint that Lotus had given the Elan new life.

£2,676 in 1971. However, this price increase, as *Autocar* pointed out, 'is hardly greater than that for the industry as a whole', and concluded that the Plus 2S 'offers standards of road behaviour which are still difficult to find elsewhere'.

Elan Sprint

A month later *Motor* took over an Elan Sprint and carried out a 'brief test'. Judged against the earlier model Elan they concluded that 'by eliminating driveshaft surge, making the exhaust quieter and giving the engine a claimed 25 per cent power increase, Lotus have succeeded in giving the car a new lease of life.' Again, we find it is the final drive which ultimately limits the car's top speed. *Motor* continues: 'So, based solely on the engine's peak revs (6,800rpm), we calculate that the Sprint is capable of 121mph (194.7kph), and probably a lot more if you're not worried about engine life.' Acceleration-wise, the Sprint could cover the 0–60mph (0–96.5kph) dash in a timed 6.7sec, which compared favourably with the 7.3sec time *Motor* recorded for the earlier Series 4 car. But they had to admit that, 'These shattering times are of course attributable to the Elan's excellent power to weight ratio. The car weighs a fraction over 14cwt (711kg) ... With this sort of performance on tap we reckon the Elan Sprint is probably one of the quickest ways of getting from A to B in Britain.'

It was the driveshaft modifications which came in for the most praise since they overcame a long-standing criticism of surge in the drivetrain which even the most experienced of drivers could not totally eliminate. 'Lotus have at last listened,' said *Motor*, 'and the latest doughnuts, which have a radial lamination, are much stiffer and you have to be very brutal to induce surge.'

Six years after its introduction there were few, if any, cars which had the same road-holding abilities as the Elan and *Motor* commented that, 'In most respects the Elan is still a leader. On dry surfaces the road-holding is outstanding; it will go round most corners faster than visibility permits.' In the wet the extra power from the Sprint engine, coupled with its light weight, could induce some nasty moments, though the quick steering was a boon, as long as the driver's reactions were quick.

One of the outstanding facets of the suspension design was the Elan's ability to cope with very poor road surfaces without the driver needing to slow down. *Motor* claimed that, 'Outstanding roadholding is coupled with a ride which in our opinion has yet to be bettered in a sports car.'

Inevitably, there were criticisms: the dashboard retained the clumsy arrangement of knobs and switches which could be confusing in haste; the pop-up headlights remained infuriatingly slow to work; and the hood, too, came in for some sharp words because it was still fiddly to erect and noisy at speed. Even so, *Motor* acknowledged the improvements Lotus had made, which included a better silencer to cut down the exhaust rasp. They noted, too, that Lotus were making a concerted effort to try to improve their reputation for reliability. They concluded 'The Sprint is certainly the best Elan we have tested and retains its position as one of the finest sports cars in the world. We were most impressed with it.'

5 Elans on Tarmac

When Lotus introduced the Elan at the London Show in late 1962 the idea that it should in any way take over from the Elite as a fixed hard-top sports racing car was unthinkable. The Elite's background, remember, began with that historic conversation between Peter Kirwan-Taylor and Colin Chapman about designing a coupe body-shell for the Lotus Eleven chassis frame to make a suitable car for entry into Le Mans 24-Hours. Chapman's reply then was that if he was going to design a fixed-head car at all he would use a clean sheet of paper and start afresh.

So, as we have already seen, the combination of Kirwan-Taylor's undoubted talent for promoting a styling concept linked to John Frayling's artistic ability to add that indefinable quality, Frank Costin's aerodynamic sense and Ron Hickman's production engineering skills produced this outstandingly pretty machine. Yet, if Lotus were to learn anything from the Elite it was that, as a car to sell in the market-place, it was hardly the most viable product. Indeed, Chapman has been quoted as saying that they lost money on each Elite sold. The next model had to be cheaper to make and more reliable once sold to the customer. Parts (especially the engine) had to be less costly to

LOTUS 26R AT A GLANCE (Lotus Type 26 Racing Series 1)

Fifty-two units were produced during 1964 season

Price	£1,654 in component form.
Body	Lightweight body laid up with less laminations than standard shell. Hard-top fitted with GRP racing seats. Pop-up type headlights used initially.
Chassis	As standard road car but with strengthened steering rack mounting and rear suspension turrets and bracing pieces to leading Y-section of chassis.
Suspension	As standard with rubber bushes but with new front wishbones to lower ride height. New rear wishbone with adjustable locating joints. Uprated springs all round, adjustable dampers and stiffer anti-roll bar. New hubs to accept 13 × 5.5 mag-alloy knock-on wheels. Splined drive shafts.
Drivetrain	Choice of 3.9:4.1 and 4.4:1 axle ratios. Limited-slip differential with alloy front section and support.
Brakes	Uprated front discs with alloy callipers and DS11 pads all round with uprated master cylinder connected to adjustable balance bar.
Engine	Cosworth Mark 15 type engine fitted with standard specification valves, main bearing caps and crankshaft. Other parts special to engine. Power output rated at 140bhp at 6,500rpm. Lotus Cortina close ratio gearbox.

While Colin Chapman was initially against the Elan being used for racing he realised that enthusiasts would race them anyway. So, he developed the Elan 26R, an early example seen here in 1963.

buy in and overall it had to be more refined. With the GRP monocoque acting as a resonance box for the mechanical and exhaust vibrations the Elite was, to say the least, noisy.

ELAN 26R

The Elan, of course, was a different car altogether because much thought had been given to sound insulation. Moreover, with its separate backbone chassis a great deal of road-derived vibration was absorbed into the frame without being passed on to the body-shell. Yet the Elan was nevertheless a Lotus and the suspension and engine design were a reflection of its pedigree. Not surprisingly, as soon as the enthusiasts got their hands on it, the Elan began to prove itself as a worthy contender on the tracks, writing its own individual chapter in the history of Lotus. Initially, Chapman was less than happy with what was happening because he had never envisaged the Elan as a potential race car. He soon realised, however, that there was little

he could do and it was not long before he hit on the notion of selling modified Elans 'off the shelf'. Thus, the 26R (Lotus Type 26, Racing) was born.

The first person to become involved with tuning the tohc Mundy-designed Lotus engine was Keith Duckworth at Cosworth. In fact, Keith and Lotus engineer Mike Costin had started extracting considerable amounts of power from the basic 998cc 105E Anglia engine, a formula Chapman had considered using in the early days of the Elan's programme. This was at a time when the programme for the Elan was structured on a par with the Healey–Sprite, but it was clear that the performance would be disappointing so the tohc idea was adopted. With the pattern for the tohc engine finalised, Cosworth began work on developing their own tuned version of the engine. By the early 1960s, Ford's cylinder block casting technology had advanced considerably, their manufacturing processes benefiting considerably from research in the States on thin wall casting. However, slight variations in wall thickness still crept in which allowed

LOTUS 26R AT A GLANCE (Lotus Type 26 Racing Series 2)

Forty-three units were produced during 1964 and 1966

Price	£1,995 in component form.
Body	As for Series 1 but with fixed headlights under plastic lenses.
Chassis	As Series 1 but with larger gussets at Y-section of chassis.
Suspension	As Series 1 but with adjustable ball joints on upper inboard locating point for front wishbones and anti-roll bar added to rear. Road wheels enlarged to 13 × 6 mag-alloys.
Drivetrain	As Series 1 but greater use of alloy castings helped reduce weight by additional 112lb (50.8kg).
Brakes	As Series 1 but with dual master cylinder.
Engine	BRM racing unit (BRM Spec. No. 84). Power output rated at 145bhp at 6,500rpm. Phase II and Phase III engines developed to produce greater power outputs available later.

JAP (who were contracted to assemble the new Lotus engine) to bore the units out to 1,558cc. The blocks with the most metal to their cylinder walls were selected for use by Cosworth who overbored them to the full specification and fitted their own high-lift camshafts, steel crankshafts and special pistons.

MODIFIED FOR RACING

As a way of getting feedback on the performance and handling of the Elan and creating interest among prospective customers, a handful of early pre-production cars were sent out to agents such as Graham Warner, boss of the Chequered Flag Garage, who subsequently used the car as the basis for a racer. However, one of the first problems he had to overcome was the fact that the Elan (unlike the Elite) was not designed to go racing! Warner's car took over the registration number LOV 1 which Warner had used previously on his very successful racing Elite. The chassis frame was strengthened around the suspension location points to cope with the greater forces imposed by the use of wide section tyres and the increased cornering speeds during racing. The steering was modified and the original suspension joints changed to rose-type joints so that the camber, caster and toe-in set-ups could be

A 1953 Lotus Mark III taken at Prescott Hillclimb a year later. Within the space of just ten years Lotus had designed and introduced the Elan which was to become a force to be reckoned with on the tracks.

Twin Stromberg carburettors fitted to an S4 drophead. Weber carburettors give the best all-round performance with 170bhp possible on full-race engines.

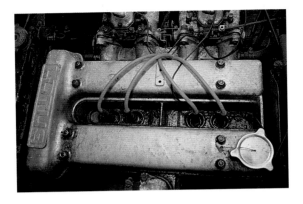

The two companies mainly associated with tuning the Lotus/Ford tohc engine were Cosworth and BRM. The performance of Weber carburettors make fitting fuel injection hardly worth the trouble and expense.

adjusted for optimum performance. Also, the original telescopic dampers were replaced by an Armstrong adjustable type. In addition, the braking system was changed to a twin circuit with two master cylinders connected by a balance bar while the actual pedals themselves were given smaller pads to improve heel-and-toe changes. To alter the effective ratio of the front to the back brakes, the rear discs were replaced by smaller ones, thereby increasing the performance of the front brakes.

Warner's Cosworth engine was fitted with the usual high-lift camshafts, racing pistons and steel crankshaft and twin 40 DCOE Webers. To improve reliability under racing conditions, the engine was assembled by hand. Many of the parts were carefully polished and balanced and items were strengthened where necessary. In this state of tune, the unit was reckoned to develop some 144bhp at 7,000 rpm. To improve airflow to the carburettors, trunking was added which married up with a NACA-type duct set in the bonnet Elite-style, while the radiator was changed to an alloy unit, located further forward in the chassis than the

original to increase the effects of the in-rush of air. An oil cooler was also fitted to improve oil viscosity. A Lotus-type close-ratio gearbox replaced the standard gearbox. The transmission of all this additional horsepower caused the Lotus driveshaft doughnuts to prove very troublesome, so universal joints and roller splines were fitted.

In November 1963 this car was tested by John Bolster of *Autosport* just before it was exported to Hong Kong. Clearly, Bolster was very impressed for he was encouraged to say of the engine's total flexibility: 'This unusual flexibility allowed Druids to be taken in second or third gear, to choice, with virtually no difference in lap times.' To conclude, Bolster said 'To handle it on a racing circuit is to experience very high performance that can be used to the full all the time.'

For 1963, Warner made do with the standard Elan soft-top, which obviously did not upset the officials, although other early Elan campaigners fitted a variety of hard-tops until Lotus themselves produced an in-house version early the following year. Another alteration made to early racing Elans was the adoption of perspex covers over small racing headlamp units in place of the

One very successful Elan driver was Pat Thomas who runs Kelvedon Motors, Lotus specialists, in Spalding, Lincolnshire. He is seen here behind the wheel of his Modsports Elan in which he won the Championship in 1981.

standard pop-up type, although those cars exported to the States retained the standard fittings. 1964 also saw the introduction of lightweight magnesium alloy road wheels and alloy fuel tanks with the body-shells being laid up using fewer laminations in an effort to reduce the weight of the car.

ELAN MANIA

During 1963, Warner's main competition came from Stirling Moss's special-bodied SMART racing team Elan driven by Sir John Whitmore, the two cars providing the racing fans with many exciting duels during the season. Only twice did the SMART car fail to finish and on both occasions the car lost a wheel. Shortly after this, alloy wheels became *de rigueur* on racing Elans. By 1964 the Elite was completely outclassed by the much faster Elans, although they still competed to good effect in the 1,300cc category. Meanwhile, the Elans were really getting into their stride with cars driven by such people as Dick Crosfield, Malcolm Wayne, Sid Taylor and John Lepp who graphically illustrated the car's prowess on the tracks. Indeed, the Ian Walker team Elan proved to be one of the most successful and was often driven by Jim Clark and Peter Arundell from the Lotus Formula team. A rising star also seen driving an Elan in the early days was Jackie Stewart. At Mallory Park in 1964, with Stewart driving Graham Warner's 26R, the finish was not surprisingly Stewart first, followed by Peter Arundell in Ian Walker's 'Gold Bug' Elan with Chris Barber's Elan driven by Mike Beckworth in third place.

Another significant Elan which appeared on the tracks during the 1964 season was the Surbiton Motors car driven by Barry Woods. In addition to the usual array of Elan racing modifications and updates, this Elan featured a full-length fastback hard-top which was permanently fixed to the main body tub. Not long after, Lotus themselves launched their own fixed hard-top coupe which bore a strong resemblance to Wood's Elan. Other Elans, too, boasted special adaptations to their bodywork; two cars worthy of mention were Moss's Ogle-designed car and John Lepp's Elan which was fitted with bodywork by Shapecraft. In the main, though, most entrants either relied on the standard soft-top (given that the scrutineers would allow it) or simply the factory's own hard-top.

By 1965 more and more enthusiasts were becoming seized by Elan mania and many well-known names were being linked with Chapman's 'luxury sports car', among them Pat Ferguson, Willie Green and Wayne and Digby Martland. John Hine proved outstandingly successful, winning the Dunlop International race at Zandvoort from Jochen Neerpasch in a similar car, while back in the UK Dick Crosfield and John Harris won the prestigious Autosport Championship in their Elan.

The editor of *Sportscar Graphic*, racing driver Gerry Titus, tested a 26R in May 1965. The roadster SCCA C-Production Elan was fitted with a 148bhp Cosworth engine and Titus found that it handled very like a Formula Junior car with almost neutral response characteristics but with a slight tendency to oversteer through slower corners. Titus also said of the car's performance that it handled so much like a mid-engined car that the driver could be fooled into wondering whether the engine really was in front!

For the 1965 round of the Autosport Championship, Crosfield teamed up with John Harris and the pair went on to win the trophy. Of the two, though, it was Harris who was the consistently faster driver. In their wake was John Hine in the Chris Barber Elan, the engine in this car producing a reputed 161.5bhp. At Zandvoort Hine's claims were confirmed when he was able to stay with the Porsche of Ben Pon and eventually passed the Elan driven by Jochen

Neerpasch to win the event. The Elan had very quickly established itself as a very competitive car providing many thrills as one chased another for the chequered flag. Every known engine tweak was used in an effort to extract that extra ounce of power to make the car go that little bit faster.

It was the same story the following year. 1966 saw the emergence of John Miles, a driver who subsequently proved himself to be one of the fastest Elan and mid-engined Lotus Europa drivers. Miles, in the Willment-prepared Elan, pulled off a brilliant season winning the Autosport Championship. However, during one memorable race in the Gold Cup meeting at Oulton Park in September, Miles managed to break his crankshaft during practice. Undaunted, he spent the night rebuilding the engine using a reconditioned block and was ready for the race the next day. After a good start, however, the water temperature began to climb, the replacement cylinder block showing its suspect history. However, by keeping the revs below his usual 7,000rpm he finished the race, although had to be content with a class win, despite giving fellow entrant E-type driver Charles Bridges some nasty moments.

Miles also had a successful drive at the Group Four race for sports cars in May earlier in the year at Oulton Park where he made the fastest time as well as winning part one of the race for cars up to 2 litres and beat two other Elan drivers, John Lepp and Julian Sutton. And Miles did it again in the second part beating the Elans of Eric Falce and Bill Dryden. In the Tulip Rally held during May, Alan Taylor and David Friswell won their class in their Ian Walker-prepared 'Gold Bug' Elan. Group Three overall winner was a Sunbeam Tiger driven by Peter Harper and Robin Turvey.

Clearly, the work which was being done on the Lotus–Cortina engine for international rallying and touring car events during this period was of great benefit to Elan develop-

ment. Experience was cross-fertilised into the Elan with the result that it became even more competitive. John Miles won ten out of the twelve events he entered as part of the Autosport Championship and gained six lap records and twelve class wins. Such domination illustrated the outstanding capabilities not only of Miles's driving but of the Elan against much bigger, more powerful machinery. In his BRM-tuned Phase Two 26R he put up some thrilling performances. One example was the Gold Cup meeting at Oulton Park in September 1966. In the GT event, Miles won his class against very stiff opposition from people such as Charles Bridges in an E-type Jaguar and Martin Hone in a Porsche 904 GTS. 1966 was, indeed, the year of the 26R.

The Boxing Day meeting at Brands Hatch saw the race début of Lotus's new 47, one of the first mid-engined sports coupes and fitted with a Lotus tohc engine. During the following year it proved to be very successful with Miles winning many of the events he entered. However, the Elan continued to produce some entertaining racing; in the supporting event at the British Grand Prix held at Silverstone in July, John Hine won his class beating fellow Elan driver Ken Simmons, while the Elans of Peter Jackson and Bill Dryden were forced to retire with mechanical problems. As for autocross, in the John Player No.6 Championship the Elans of Peter Watkins and Jeff Smith gave a good account of themselves, Watkins finally beating Smith in the run-off.

MODSPORTS

By 1970, the Production Sports Car series was seeing a whole new batch of highly modified sports cars being raced — cars which really bore no resemblance to their production origins. It was nothing to see glass-fibre-bodied MG Midgets with all-independent suspension and spaceframe

chassis out-performing much bigger engined machines. In an effort to redress the balance, the rules were changed so that such extreme alterations would no longer be allowed, the extent to which the car could be modified being clearly identified. The series was known as Modsports (events for modified sports cars), for which the Elan was ideally suited in the 2-litre class. Its lightweight chassis, lack of excess loading and highly acclaimed suspension layout were all factors in its favour. Norman Cuthbert won the class in a 26R (showing the continuing competitiveness of this factory-modified version of the Elan), while John Sabour won the Autosport Three Hour race at Snetterton in his

An Elan Sprint with flared wheelarches (left and below). *By the time the Sprint was introduced in 1971 the Elan had already gained an enviable reputation with drivers such as Ken Miles who dominated the* Autosport *Championship in 1966.*

Ian Walker-prepared Elan. John Fletcher, in a highly modified Elan, also illustrated the car's prowess in events in the north of England.

However, it was not only in racing that the Elan made its mark. Jeff Goodliffe, director of British Vita Racing, won the British Automobile Racing Club's Hillclimb Championship in a highly modified Elan which even featured Chevron Formula 3 parts. The road section of the same championship was also won by an Elan with Ricky Gould at the wheel. With the change in race car preparation rules in 1970 — after several years out in the wilderness when it was outclassed by the mid-engined Lotus 47s and Chevron B8s — the Elan once more found itself in favour. The Norman Cuthbert Elan (the car which had been campaigned by Bill Dryden to win the Autosport Championship in 1967) based on a 26R was tested by Richard Hudson-Evans in the October issue of *Cars and Car Conversions*. Among the modifications was an engine, prepared by Alan Smith, which reputedly produced 170bhp. The gearbox was the extremely tough 'Bullet' close ratio Ford gearbox driving a Hewland limited-slip differential and Minilite 8in wide front and 8.5in wide rear alloy wheels. Hudson-Evans found a considerable amount of understeer with this car which demanded that the driver use increasing amounts of lock to get round corners. However, a somewhat distressing effect (which seemed most pronounced during braking) was the Elan competition 'weave'. Hudson-Evans made the point that it became most noticeable if he gripped the wheel too tightly and said that he felt that at times the car had a 'directional mind of its own'. After the test, talks with Cuthbert concluded that this rather worrying phenomenon could have been the combination of bump steer and chassis flexing. (A case of too much power for the car, perhaps?)

The following year the Goodliffe Elan was taken over by Dave Brodie who fitted a monster 2.1-litre Cosworth BDA engine and spent a considerable amount of effort perfecting the suspension set-up. However, Fletcher's Elan continued to prove highly competitive, winning the title in the STP Modsports Championship. Meanwhile, Max Payne (who had spent some time trying to campaign a +2, but its greater weight was not fully off-set by the increased handling produced by its wider track) bought Norman Cuthbert's Elan.

In 1971, it was the same story, with Elans to the fore as before. Fletcher came very close to winning the STP Modsports Championship and succeeded in the Chevron Oils series. In contrast, the John Sabourin Elan was rebuilt with sponsorship from VRM for Dave Brodie who unfortunately crashed it again! Other Elans also performed well including Max Payne's (which was now running on a 1.8-litre engine), and those of Mick Nugent, Donald Morton and Brian Ashwood, which all gained class wins.

In 1976 Fletcher won his class in the BRSCC series for Modsports cars. The British Automobile Racing Club (BARC) events allowed more extreme machines to compete, thereby making the Elan less competitive, although Fletcher did succeed in this round the following year. He took the BRSCC Championship, too, sharing the winner's laurels with fellow Elan driver David Mercer. For 1977, Mercer took to driving an MG Midget but Fletcher, true to Lotus, continued with the Chapman machine and managed to take both the BRSCC and the BARC Modsports championships — despite increasingly tough opposition from the Elans of Paul Berman and Max Payne. Clearly the Elan was proving popular in most areas of competitive motor sport, particularly the Clubman's series of Modsports in which it proved to be highly successful with such people as John Sabourin, Norman Cuthbert and most especially, John Fletcher. One Elan which proved to be outstandingly quick and which won its début race was the lightweight car – it weighed just 1,000lb (453.6kg) – prepared by Victor Raysbrook Motors for Dave Brodie to drive. It was later campaigned by Gerry Marshall during 1973 and then by John Pearson who, despite great opposition, won four races in succession.

PRODSPORTS

1973 also saw the introduction of Prodsports (events for production sports cars) in which the rules clearly indicated the extent of the modifications. Meanwhile, in Modsports, the Elans continued their competitive spirit and John Fletcher, in particular, proved to be very quick during the 1975 season. In the Classic Car series, the Elan of John Webb (a London-based Lotus salesman with sponsorship from Rochas) proved to be very successful driving the ex-Eric Oliver car. Another old adversary of Fletcher's was Paul Berman who, in May 1979, won the British Racing Sports Car Club's Modsports Championship at Brands Hatch. Despite gaining pole position from practice, Berman made a bad start but quickly made up to take a lead he never relinquished. Alas, John Fletcher's Elan retired with a broken throttle cable. Another Elan to show its colours was the Max Payne and John Evans car. A Group Five machine, it suffered a bottom wishbone mounting failure during the ninth round of the World Championship of Makes at Brands Hatch in August, giving Evans a nasty moment.

In March 1965, *Small Car* were able to get their hands on Stirling Moss's SMART racing Elan for an evaluation drive on normal roads. 'And since Colin Chapman's chaotic empire in Hertfordshire had consistently failed to deliver the test cars it kept promising, we jumped at the chance when *Small Car* contributor Moss offered us a weekend with the car . . .', they said.

The car was about to be sold to the Motor Racing Stables at Brands Hatch, so this was an ideal opportunity for the people from *Small Car* magazine to get their hands on a blood-tingling racing Elan. It was not, however, all praise for the SMART team because *Small Car*'s motor noter listed a whole catalogue of problems, not least of which was that the chassis frame had proved to be 'too flimsy to cope with the shocks transmitted to it from the drastically lowered and tightened suspension'. (Perhaps that is why the great man at Lotus had said, '. . . the Elan isn't suitable for racing.') In addition, the specially-made lightweight glass-fibre body had progressively fallen to bits and other accessories (just what, they did not say) had stopped working at inconvenient times.

However, despite these shortcomings, it was clear that the car did perform very quickly indeed, *Small Car* registering a 0–60mph (0–96.5kph) sprint of 7.1sec, going on to 100mph (160.93kph) in 17sec. Top-class Lotus engine exponent Keith Duckworth had managed to extract 153bhp from the 1,600cc engine. While Birmingham traffic jams did nothing for the water temperature, reducing the unit to fluffing its plugs (it was a sports racing car, after all), on the open road it was an altogether different story. The suspension set-up was clearly very harsh and unforgiving on anything other than smooth surfaces. Indeed, the ride was so spine-jarring that at one stage *Small Car* felt that the wheels were actually bolted directly to the chassis. That said, there was no roll whatsoever on corners, the only limiting factor here being the range of the driver's visibility! The brakes, too, were certainly up to standard. The only major disadvantage, it seems, was the enormous amount of heat from the engine which permeated through to the cockpit. At one stage the occupants were forced to drive along with the doors open in an effort to reduce the sauna-like atmosphere in the interior – and this despite the fact that the hard-top had no windows other than front and rear screens!

Taking the engine out to 1,800cc and fitting 45 DCOE Weber carburettors along with a high-lift camshaft and modified cylinder head it is possible to extract around 180bhp from the tohc engine.

LOTUS JOIN THE FIELD

By 1964 Lotus's attitude towards leaping on the Elan sports racing car bandwagon had changed markedly as an extract from their Lotus 26R brochure illustrates:

'The standard Lotus Elan produced by Lotus Cars Ltd. is a production high performance luxury sports car designed to give the owner value on a money to performance basis hitherto unequalled in a small capacity market. It is not suitable for racing . . .'

To satisfy the insatiable appetites of those enthusiasts who wanted to race, Lotus Components Ltd. began marketing the *very*

special 26R and Peter Westbury took delivery of the first car on 20 March 1964. Thereafter, some fifty-one Series 1 cars were supplied before the Series 2 version was introduced. Forty-one of these were built before production ceased and the last car dispatched on 23 July 1966. When it was new the 26R was homologated into Group Four in which the rules state that the manufacturer was required to build 100 cars. Very shrewdly, Lotus homologated the standard road car listing most of the components as being 'modified' and, in doing so, allowed a free rein for any future alterations.

To assemble the 26R, Lotus Components used the basic Elan chassis frame but added strengthening plates to the leading edge of the chassis fork and the rear suspension uprights. These strengthening modifications were beefed-up for the Series 2 version. At the front, the standard ball joints and bushes were retained, although the wishbones were changed to lower the ride height. The hubs were changed to take the 13 × 5.5in knock-on alloy road wheels, while the springs and anti-roll bar were uprated and the dampers changed to adjustable type. At the rear, the wishbones were given adjustable joints and, like the front, the springs were uprated with adjustable dampers with hubs to take the knock-on alloy wheels. To overcome the wind-up problem in the Rotaflex drive couplings, these were replaced with heavy-duty roller spline shafts and universal joints. The differential front end and carrier were made from light alloy and the limited-slip unit could be supplied in a choice of ratios – 4.44:1, 4.1:1 and 3.9:1. The brakes were uprated, too, with alloy callipers and special discs and DS11 pads operated from an uprated master cylinder.

For the Series 1 car, Lotus followed Warner's choice by offering the potent Cosworth Mark 15 engine which developed around 140bhp at 6,500rpm. Surprisingly,

the crankshaft, main bearing caps and valves were from the standard specification tohc Lotus engine although, as with the Warner car, considerable effort was made to strengthen or change vulnerable components, the whole unit being carefully assembled. Carburation utilised twin 40 DCOE-2s with a four-branch exhaust manifold.

Price-wise, in 1964 the standard Elan cost £1,095 while the 26R cost a substantial £1,645 in component form. A long-range fuel tank was an extra £27. Within twelve months the price had jumped to £1,995 (compared to the road car's £1,179 price tag in customer completion form). But this price rise did reflect an increased number of modifications included in the standard 26R specification. To begin with, the engines were now supplied by BRM instead of Cosworth, although the gearbox was still the Lotus–Cortina-type 'Bullet' box. Underneath, the rubber-based joints on the front upper inboard suspension were changed to adjustable rose joints and to further improve handling an anti-roll bar was added to the rear. The brakes were changed to dual circuit

When developing a race engine to produce high power levels it is essential to assemble the engine with care.

Although some people went racing with the original pop-up headlights in place many opted for small racing lights beneath clear perspex covers.

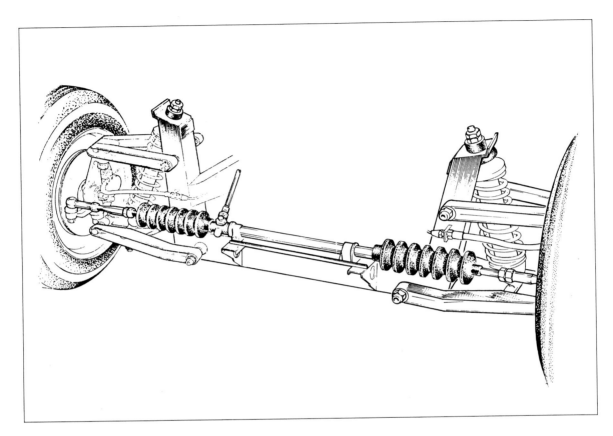

Layout of steering and front suspension.

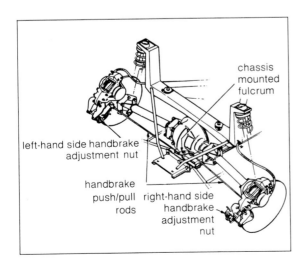

chassis
mounted
fulcrum

left-hand side handbrake
adjustment nut

handbrake
push/pull
rods

right-hand side
handbrake
adjustment
nut

Handbrake mechanism.

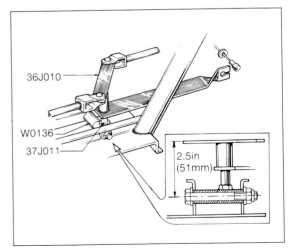

36J010

W0136

37J011

2.5in
(51mm)

*Handbrake linkage and actuating
rods assembly.*

with alloy callipers all round and the wheels were increased in width to 6in. The body was an untrimmed lightweight shell with a hard-top to satisfy the scrutineers and the pop-up headlights were replaced by small racing lamps with perspex covers. Inside, the trim was non-existent with simply a racing-type bucket seat. As production got under way, further efforts were made to save weight by using an alloy radiator with a separate header tank and a racing Varley battery. However, the records show that while performance was vastly increased over the road-going Elan, this weight-saving work had little overall effect.

Despite its Ford-based origin and the difficulties experienced in the early days regarding the poor quality of the cylinder head castings, the Lotus tohc engine must by now be recognised as one of the most successful road/race production engines ever. The basic design was so right that no fundamental modifications have to be made for a racing version, the only variations being in the choice of special components – and even then the choice is limited.

Over the years, many well-known people have spent a considerable amount of time race-tuning the tohc engine, their differing experiences and preferences leading them to rely on a particular method of extracting that little bit of extra power. However, it is generally acknowledged that it was Keith Duckworth who started the development ball rolling with this engine by identifying the need for race-based parts and where those parts were most needed. Such items as crankshaft, pistons, rods and main bearing caps were changed for steel equivalents and the cylinder head was gas flowed to improve the engine's 'breathing'. In this state of tune, fitted with twin 40 DCOE Weber carburettors, power output was rated at 140–145bhp at 7,000rpm.

All went well with Cosworth supplying Lotus with uprated engines for the first generation of 26Rs. However, at a luncheon given by Champion in honour of the Lord Mayor's Show, Colin Chapman just happened to be seated next to Tony Rudd of BRM. Suffice it to say that subsequently there was an agreement whereby BRM would take over supplying modified engines. Just what the reasons were for Chapman's decision to involve BRM at this stage is obviously open to conjecture. Perhaps it was simply that he felt it would be beneficial to bring in another opinion and it also meant that he did not have to rely solely on Cosworth.

As it was, BRM supplied the great majority of race-tuned engines for the 26R, as well as for the Lotus–Cortina and Lotus 47s. An assembly pattern was put in place which involved sending cylinder blocks and heads to BRM's headquarters in Bourne where the heads were gas flowed, and over-sized valves and high-lift camshafts fitted. The blocks were overbored to 1,594cc with special rods, pistons and crankshafts installed. In this state of tune with twin 40 DCOE carburettors, the engines produced around 160bhp. They were then sent to Lotus Components at Cheshunt for installation into chassis units.

Despite the intense reliability and tuning development programme involving both the Cheshunt and the Cosworth teams, BRM still experienced problems with head gasket failure at high revs. The immediate solution was to use cylinder heads cast by Aeroplane & Motor Ltd. and, with different material used in the manufacture of the head gaskets, the problems were reduced. However, the long term answer was to use sandcast heads produced by William Mills.

In addition to those engines which were assembled for delivery to Lotus, BRM also offered four stages of tune for the Elan ranging from 130–140bhp, 140+bhp,

The much-modified Elan of Lotus specialists Kelvedon Motors (overleaf). Notice how the whole car has been altered by the removal of the sills.

160bhp and 175+bhp, the latter version utilising fuel injection. Early on, the Lucas mechanical system was used, however, this proved very unsatisfactory because there was no metering device to control the flow of fuel into the combustion chambers, so it was dropped in favour of the Tecalemit Jackson-type. Unfortunately, unreliability remained a problem so Weber carburettors were employed once more, giving away only 5bhp in the process. Generally, it is considered that while BRM's camshaft design and cylinder head gas flowing was in advance of that offered by Cosworth, the choice of parts used in the assembly of BRM engines was almost over-kill in terms of their strength. Cosworth's all-steel components resulted in a more efficient rotating mass.

ROAD TEST: ELAN BRM

In a road test carried out on a soft-top Elan prepared by BRM, tester Patrick McNally said:

'The BRM version is basically the same with the exception of its high performance engine, specially developed by the BRM division of Rubery Owen, which gives the car a maximum speed of 130mph (209.2kph) and a 0–60 time comparable with an E-type Jaguar or a DB6 Vantage Aston Martin.'

The car tested was in full road trim and, indeed, proved to be just as flexible as the standard machine. The unit had been modified in the usual fashion at BRM's headquarters: the head was gas flowed with bigger valves and the surface machined to increase compression rates and to correct variations in tolerance; the crankshaft was balanced and tougher Ford C-type rods fitted bigger jets were used in the twin Weber carburettors; and a 'special' exhaust system completed the package.

'But the effect of 130bhp changes the whole nature of the car' commented McNally, and continued to say that 'The roadholding is still first class, but much more fun can be experienced as the car can be driven far more on the throttle and requires more skill and handling.'

Using 7,000rpm (the limiting device had been removed) 0–60mph (0–96.5kph) time was recorded as 6.8sec with a 0–100mph (0–160.9kph) dash of a most creditable 18.2sec. McNally also made the point that while he reckoned this to be a true 130mph (209.2kph) car, with a higher final drive ratio this speed could be bettered. In addition, 'the BRM-tuned power unit also encouraged the most enthusiastic cornering techniques as there is sufficient power available to sort out any difficulties.' Clearly, a most remarkable machine since not only was it very fast but the fuel consumption was calculated to be around 25mpg (40.2kpg). What DB6 Vantage Aston Martin-owner could laugh that off?

ROAD TEST: VITA RACING ELAN

To get a measure of the background of one of the most successful racing Elans which was to be seen during the early 1970s, *Motor Sport* tested Richard Lloyd's Elan which was campaigned to such great effect by Dave Brodie with sponsorship provided by the Gold Seal Sports Car Centre in South London. At the time of the test it was the lap record holder for the club circuit at Brands Hatch with six club wins to its credit in the Modsports series. The car was originally built by Jeff Goodliffe, Director of the British Vita Racing Team based in Littleborough, Lancashire and won the 1970 Castrol-BARC Hillclimb Championship. Although the car used a smaller engine during its Goodliffe days, it did receive one rather extensive modification, that of being fitted with Chevron formula

Another view of Pat Thomas at Silverstone in 1977.

racing front brakes which involved the fabrication of a special cradle which interfaced between the Lotus chassis and the Chevron uprights and hub/disc assembly.

All round, the brakes utilised Girling alloy callipers with adjustable dampers (Koni on the front and Armstrong on the rear), with slightly uprated racing coil springs with adjustable suspension joints and 8.5in Minilite alloy wheels with Dunlop 350 racing tyres. When the car passed into Lloyd's hands much time and effort was spent in setting up the suspension for racing so that it would be possible for Brodie to conduct it round corners at a potential 110mph (177kph). Much more fundamental, though, was the decision to fit a larger capacity engine, the replacement being a full 1,974cc which was achieved by using an all-new cylinder block, rods and a Gordon Allen steel crankshaft giving a bore and stroke of 90mm × 77.62mm. The pistons had to be machined from blanks, the machining being undertaken by the Hanwell-based firm of Hillthorne Engineering while the actual

assembly was taken care of by Racing Services of Twickenham. The cylinder head was an original British Vita Racing Team part with a compression ratio of 12.5:1. When it was put on the brake after Racing Services had finished their handiwork, it was found to produce an impressive 178bhp at 6,800rpm. The gearbox was a standard Ford 'Bullet' box driving a 3.9 final drive with a Salisbury limited-slip, and Ford Zodiac UJs linked to Brabham F2 driveshafts. Inside, the car was remarkably standard for a full race machine — even down to the road-going electric windows. (It was perhaps a shame that the radio had to go to make room for a chrono-metric rev counter.)

Under test the car was found to be remarkably easy to handle with no apparent vices and after just fifteen laps came the best-timed circuit of 1min 6.4sec (compared to 1min 4.6sec which was the class record).

Despite Chapman's reluctance in the early days to agree to the Elans being raced, the car continues to be a very competitive club racing machine. This surely says a lot for the original design.

6 Under the Microscope

Because of its design, performance and just out-and-out flair, it is sometimes easy to forget that the average Elan is now well over twenty years old. Indeed, the very youngest used model you are ever likely to look at will be an amazing seventeen years old – almost out of its teens! The same applies to the bigger +2 range.

It goes without saying that the true innovative genius of Chapman's design engineering was never more evident than in the Elan. Its concept was so far ahead of its time that, even in 1989/1990, manufacturers are still trying to emulate its small, agile and impressively comfortable characteristics. It comes as no surprise, then, that with the current trend in classic cars as an investment, the Elan (although less so for the +2, at least for the moment) is one marque whose values have risen dramatically.

In an effort to simplify the process of buyer spot checks, it is as well at this point to reflect for a moment on the purpose of the purchase and, equally importantly, the amount of money available. Almost certainly, the three major purchase/use categories to be considered are:

1. A car which has been fully restored by a reputable company like Daytune of Cambridge or Patrick Thomas of Spalding, the car being almost 'as new'. Inevitably, however, such a purchase will be very expensive and in the main such Elans are bought as fun cars to be used rarely – and then only during the summer months.
2. The car which can best be described as in 'good overall condition'. It will either be for sale in a garage which deals in Lotus cars or it will be the pride and joy of its current owner. It may have a replacement chassis and almost certainly the engine will have had some work done to it at one time or another. Such a car could make good everyday transport – with a bit of care and attention – though the amount of money available to make the purchase will ultimately limit the condition of the car.
3. The restoration project. The purchase will form the basis for a hobby which could keep its new owner occupied for many months to come for, without doubt, it will involve a chassis-off rebuild. Clearly, the ground rules for this sort of purchase are very different from those of the first and second categories, although there are still some basic points to be considered when choosing a likely candidate.

However, these categories aside, for the majority of people the most important factor to be kept in mind is the amount of money available. This, more than anything else, will determine the car's condition at the time of purchase and the speed at which a restoration programme will progress if plans are to rebuild the car. Needless to say, things always cost more than is originally planned. But even before reaching for the calculator to work out the cash situation, think about the benefits to be gained from joining one of the Lotus clubs. It makes sense to become a member of a club which specialises in the car you intend to buy. Attend a few of the club meetings, talk to other enthusiasts and begin to get a grasp of the sort of problems they encountered. You may even find someone close to your home who will come along with you to look over a car you intend to buy. Benefiting from other people's experience, free of charge, cannot be bad!

Perhaps the most important rule of all — and one which applies to the purchase of *any* classic car — is always to buy the most expensive car you can afford but leave a little money in hand for running costs. It goes without saying that even the day-to-day running costs of an Elan or +2 will be more than those for an MGB or Triumph Spitfire. The Elan was and is a very fast sports car and insurance is an area to be looked at carefully. The Elan's image and fibreglass body mean that insurance will be heavily loaded so it is worth shopping around. That said, the insurance ought to be from a reputable company and an agreed value comprehensive cover policy of the type specifically designed for classic cars. Like road fund tax it is one of the constant costs of running a car which have to be found each year.

Mike Kimberley, Colin Chapman and Tony Rudd discussing design details round a drawing board. The fact that the Elan and the Plus 2 are so attractive to the enthusiast is mainly due to the talents of these three men.

LOTUS ELAN AND ELAN PLUS 2 – Buyer's Spot Checks

Body	Cracking and crazing of GRP. Wear in door hinges. Rips and holes in canvas of soft-top version.
Chassis	Rust in front and rear suspension turrets, engine crossmember, and differential carrier. Stress cracks at apexes of chassis forks (especially on Plus 2).
Suspension	Geometry out-of-true caused by accident. Wear in all rubber bushes and front trunion joints. Cracks in rear drive shaft (Rotaflex) couplings. Wear in wheel bearings and steering rack bushes.
Drivetrain	Oil leakage and wear in differential. Dragging clutch action. Wear in propeller shaft (especially on Plus 2).
Brakes	Warped or scored brake discs. Damaged hydraulic hoses.
Engine	Traces of oil and water leakage. Worn or broken engine mountings. Noise from timing gear and lack of adjustment on chain tensioner. Wear in water pump bearing. Oil pressure (20psi at idle) and degree of 'smoking'. Engine running temperature (90–100°C). Wear in gearbox bearings and synchromesh.

Another point to keep in mind is the availability of a reasonable garage – not only for keeping the car in, but also so that the frequent maintenance checks which these cars demand can be done in adequate comfort. Then the location of the nearest Lotus agent should be considered. If you are a DIY enthusiast it is as well to forward plan on stocks of parts for servicing, although this will be covered in greater detail later. That said, Lotus are better served than many other classic cars when it comes to the number of specialist agents throughout the country. It is possible, of course, to buy some spares that will fit an Elan or +2 from other factors, but if you are going to keep the car in tip-top running condition – and keep it original – it is best to buy Lotus parts. Moreover, there are a few jobs which really *are* best left to the professionals if the car is to be kept at its peak.

BUYING: THE 'AS NEW' CAR

Starting with our first category of prospective purchase, clearly if you are going to buy a fully restored car from one of the highly-respected specialists, then the only real considerations are the price, the extent of the restoration, the after-sales service and what is covered by the warranty and for how long. If the car has been totally restored from the chassis up, then in most respects it must be considered to be an 'as new' car.

BUYING: FOR THE ROAD

Moving on to the second category, we will assume that the car will be bought through one of the 'for sale' columns for classic cars, the main criteria here being age, price and condition. After deciding upon what appears to be a suitable candidate, most experts agree that the wisest move is to arrange with the owner to take it along to one of the Lotus specialists who offer a purchase inspection/report service. The bonus of this kind of check-over is that it is unbiased and carried out by people who themselves have a reputation to uphold. Moreover, their years of experience will be invaluable when judging the degree of wear and whether it is acceptable.

If it is not practical to subject the car to this sort of inspection an alternative is to take along a friend from the club. Go along armed with some ramps and a good quality jack (ideally a trolley jack). Make the appoint-

CHASSIS IDENTIFICATION

Date	Chassis number	Comment
January 1963	26/0001	Elan 1500 introduced
May 1963	26/0026	Hard-top optional
January 1964	26/0330	Model continues
November 1964	26/3901	Series 2 introduced
January 1965	26/4325	Series 2 continues
September 1965	36/4510	Series 3 fhc introduced
November 1965	36/5147	Close ratio gearbox available
January 1966	26/5207	Convertible continues
	36/5201	Fhc continues
	26/5282	Special Equipment convertible available
June 1966	26/5810	S2 convertible final chassis number
	26/5798	S2 convertible (Special Equipment) final chassis number
	45/5702	S3 convertible introduced
	45/5701	S3 convertible (Special Equipment) introduced
July 1966	36/5977	S3 fhc (Special Equipment) introduced
January 1967	45/6678	S3 convertible continued
	45/6680	S3 convertible (Special Equipment) continued
	36/6679	S3 fhc continued
	36/6683	S3 fhc (Special Equipment) continued
June 1967	50/0001	+2 fhc introduced
August 1967	45/7328	Convertible continued
	45/7329	Convertible (Special Equipment) continued
	36/7327	Fhc continued
	36/7331	Fhc (Special Equipment) continued
March 1968	45/7895	S4 convertible introduced
	36/7895	S4 fhc introduced
November 1968	50/1280	Stromberg carbs introduced on +2 fhc
	45/8600	Stromberg carbs introduced on convertible
	45/8600	Stromberg carbs introduced on fhc
March 1969	50/1554	+2 fhc introduced
August 1969	45/9524	Weber carbs re-introduced on convertible
	36/9524	Weber carbs re-introduced on fhc
December 1969	50/2407	+2 final chassis number
	50/2536	Final number of old numbering (Plus 2S)
	45/9824	Final number of old numbering (convertible)
	36/9824	Final number of old numbering (fhc)
January 1970	7001 010001	All models continued with a suffix to identify each one, for example S4 fhc=A; S4 fhc (Special Equipment)=E; S4 convertible=C; S4 convertible (Special Equipment)=G; Plus 2S fhc=L.7001=1970 January
February 1971	7101	Sprint version introduced on fhc and convertible; Plus 2S 130 introduced
January 1972	7201	Models continue unchanged
October 1972	—	Five-speed gearbox optional on Plus 2S 130
January 1973	7301	Convertible and fhc continued
	7301 1132	Plus 2S 130 and Plus 2S 130/5 continued
August 1973	7301	Elan convertible and fhc discontinued

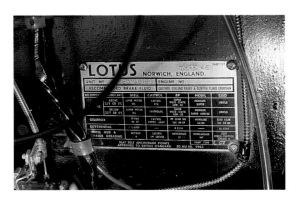

When looking at a potential car it is worth checking the specification plate. Some unscrupulous vendors have been known to sell a 'bitsa' as an Elan Sprint, so be warned.

ment for mid-morning or early afternoon. People who have bought cars in the dark have sometimes lived to regret it. And remember that the majority of the major checks you will be making will be under the car not around it, so be prepared and take a pair of overalls! At the outset, make a note of the car's chassis number. This is particularly important if the car is purported to be a Sprint (either hard-top or roadster). Check the chassis number against the known chassis numbers of the Sprint production run – the outcome might be interesting! (*See* Chassis Identification table, page 115.)

As has been discussed in previous pages, the core construction of the Elan and the +2 is a backbone chassis for which both cars

And while you're about it look to see if the car still has its original tool kit and handbook. It all indicates whether the previous owner has looked after the car.

Chapman's delightful backbone chassis. This is the +2 version with wider track to take account of the broader body-shell. It is easy to see how water can get trapped, causing severe corrosion.

ultimately became famous. However, they also became infamous as the years rolled on for the degree to which these chassis structures could become the subject of severe rot. In the early days, Chapman's long-term weather proofing left much to be desired. He was not alone in this — in the 1960s and early 1970s most other car manufacturers were equally guilty. Close inspection of the car will reveal that the basic design of the chassis is a folded sheet steel design which is a top hat in section. At all four corners, square section steel turrets are welded on to give the necessary height to accommodate the

suspension struts. With the car up on ramps it is possible to begin a detailed inspection of the condition of the chassis — to do this you should begin with the front.

The two main reasons for chassis damage are rust and accident or suspension wear which has caused the metal to be twisted out of alignment. Over the years a corrosive mixture of water, salt and mud will have found the possible traps in the chassis design. Clearly, this causes a gradual weakening of the turrets and the main chassis frame itself with dangerous results. Equally possibly, the car may have been involved in an accident at

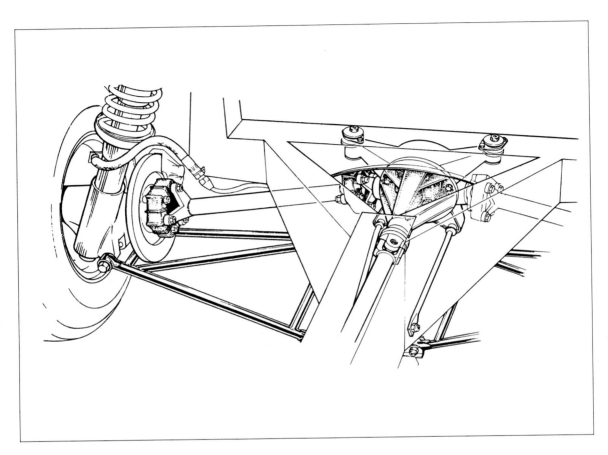

Final drive arrangement.

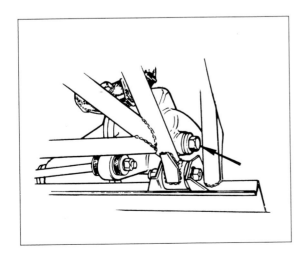

Filler/level plug.

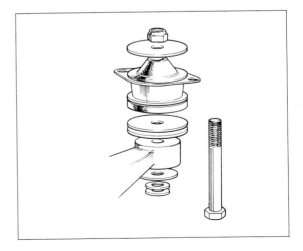

Washer sequence.

some time in its life which may have twisted the chassis with dire effects on suspension geometry. Also, wear in the suspension struts can mean that the dampening effect is almost totally destroyed, allowing the struts to 'bottom' on the top of the turret. This continuous hammering of metal on metal causes damage to the suspension mounting.

Rust in the chassis or turrets can often be spotted immediately, although it should also be remembered that in most cases any rust will be acting from the inside outwards so the outer surface of the chassis is the last place it will make itself known. A tip is to be on the look-out for fresh applications of underseal! Unfortunately, accurate chassis checks to reveal any inaccuracies in suspension alignment are not easy for the amateur although in bad cases a line-of-sight inspection of front and rear wheels can sometimes indicate that all is not well. Another possible clue is uneven tyre wear. The fact is that only in exceptional cases will the original chassis of a twenty-year-old Lotus still be in good condition. (That said, it is still possible to preserve an original Elan chassis by keeping a constant eye on its condition and regular cleaning and clearing of the drain holes.) Welding in plates to repair rot on a damaged chassis section is *not* to be recommended. The best answer is always a complete replacement chassis. These days, Lotus replacement chassis for both the Elan and the +2 are fully galvanised and stamped 'LR' for Lotus Replacement.

So, if inspections indicate the presence of rot (to say nothing of what cannot be seen) should the car be discarded? Almost certainly, yes – unless its price is such that it takes account of the cost of putting things right. Even then, be aware that although old hands will pass off a chassis replacement job as a straightforward, albeit lengthy, task it is hardly something which should be tackled lightly by anyone new to Lotus. Not only that, but any chassis replacement programme should also take in a suspension and

brake overhaul, replacing all pipes and bushes in the process. Is the car really worth all that?

The next area to look at while under the car is the suspension locating bushes. Chapman used rubber bushes everywhere in a conscious effort to reduce noise and vibration. These tend to dry and crack over a period of time while those which have been covered in oil will perish. (If the bush is covered in oil, also ask yourself where the oil is coming from.) Between the outer ends of the bottom wishbones Lotus used Triumph-based nylon bushes or trunions and these do wear very quickly. That said, if wear has been identified in any of these areas do not be put off since bushes and trunions are easy and cheap to replace.

While you are under the front of the car look at the condition of the front cross-member which can also become rotten. Then move on to the steering rack. The rack was mounted in rubber bushes which can easily become covered in engine or steering rack oil. Check these, as well as the gaiters at both ends of the rack which cover the bushes holding the track-rod ends. Loss of oil from the rack can cause excessive wear in these bushes so inspect for excess play in the track-rod ends where they leave the steering-rack casing. While it is certainly true that the rack is originally from the Triumph parts bin, it was modified by Lotus so a replacement rack *must* be a Lotus unit. Finally, take a careful look at the condition of the brake pipes and hoses, as well as the brake discs.

Engine mountings, too, can become covered in oil or damaged through working themselves loose and, in turn, become elongated from wear. Also, hairline stress cracks can begin to appear in the 'Y' formation of the chassis frame.

Next, put the rear of the car up on ramps to inspect the final drive and driveshaft couplings. Indication of a slight oil leak from the differential is reckoned to be acceptable

The bonnet lid of this Elan has been removed to make the job of checking over the engine that much easier. The fuel pump and distributor are hidden beneath the Weber carburettors.

The boot-mounted battery. Check to ensure that the electrolyte has not leaked with disastrous results.

Some Elans were fitted with twin Stromberg carburettors. For the DIY enthusiast adjustment was easier than with the more usual Webers.

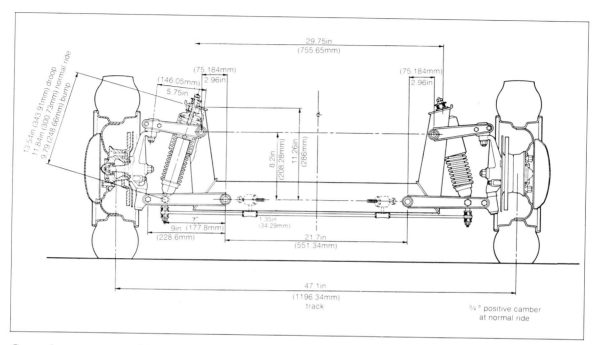

General arrangement of front suspension.

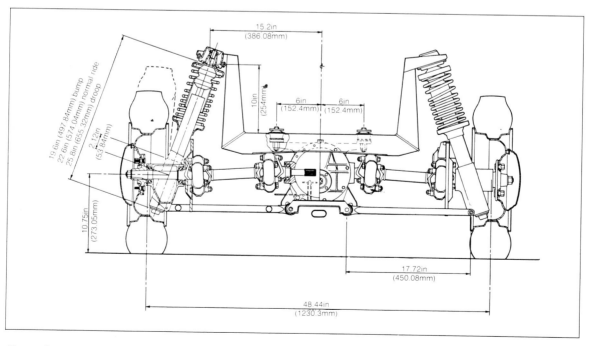

General arrangement of rear suspension.

— even preferred since it protects the rear of the chassis structure — but, clearly, it should be limited to traces of oil tears running down the casing and not large drops leaving a mess on the ground!

As with the front section of the chassis, be aware of rot in the suspension turrets or plates which have been welded in to form make-shift repairs. As for the driveshaft couplings or doughnuts, these are a fundamental characteristic of the Elan and +2, their design being modified over the years in an effort to make them tougher and more able to transmit the greater and greater amounts of torque produced by the Lotus tohc engine. Even if the car is driven with care over the years the rubber will begin to deteriorate with traces of cracking around the steel bushes which take the locating bolts. In very bad cases the entire coupling can simply break up. The lifespan for these units can vary from 3,000 miles (4,828km) if the driver shows no concern whatsoever for his car, to around 40,000 miles (64,372km) if the car is driven gently. Wear in the prop shaft universal joints is another point to check. Remember that in order to handle the increased torque, additional strengthening struts were added to the Sprint chassis mounting points for the final drive. These can also act as verification that the car really is what its owner claims! Cracks can also begin around the mountings for the final-drive torque rods and look, too, for cracks in the final-drive casing itself.

Finally, as with the front, look carefully at the condition of the brake pipes and fuel line. While it is true that these are MoT check points, a lot can happen in twelve months and it is a good thing to know their condition anyway. Inspect, too, for signs of scoring on the rear brake discs.

Next, jack the car up a side at a time leaving the road wheels on for a moment to check for wheel bearing condition. This can be done by rocking the wheel vertically and noting the degree of movement. At the front,

it is also possible to see whether there is any wear in the swivel joints, while the condition of the steering joints can be further judged by moving the wheel to and fro horizontally. Finally, remove the road wheel and inspect the condition of the brake pipes and the outer surfaces of the brake discs for cracking and scores. Keeping some sort of notation of the problems you have found and a rough note of the cost involved in rectifying them might be worthwhile as you go round. Remember, too, that the chassis and sill sections on the Plus 2 should be thoroughly checked because these are important for the car's rigidity.

With the car standing four-square back on its wheels it is time to look under the bonnet. There is a school of thought which says that you should look out for a recently cleaned engine as this indicates a hurried repair. Equally, most enthusiasts can admire a well-looked-after engine which has been regularly degreased with one of the proprietary cleaning agents. The truth is, however, how many cars do you see which are like this when you are looking for a car to buy?

The best way to check the engine is to run it until it is thoroughly warm so that everything is at its working tolerance and the oil is at its normal viscosity. Over the years, the Lotus tohc engine seems to have gained a reputation for poor reliability. In fact, Lotus themselves never had a single warranty claim on this engine which would appear to bear out the maxim that in the right hands these units can be assembled to give many years (say 70,000+ miles or 112,651km) of use before a rebuild is required. Perhaps what is closer to the truth is that they are a meddler's paradise, so-called 'experts' often applying misplaced confidence to an engine which needs a little more knowledge than is normally required to maintain that of, say, a Healey–Sprite or Triumph Spitfire. Suffice it to say that the Ford-based Lotus engine, when overhauled by someone who knows what he is about, can give good, trouble-free service with only the usual periodic attention and adjustment necessary to keep it running properly.

Lotus engines do have a reputation for being oil leakers, the oil managing to escape either from around the cam cover retaining bolts or from beneath the cam cover gaskets themselves. If this can be identified as being *the* cause of the leak then fine, a gasket change with the proper Senloc washers is all that is required to put matters right. If the oil appears to be escaping from somewhere else though, an engine strip down might well be the only cure.

The Lotus engine has also grown up with a reputation for having a thirst for water pump bearings. The complexity of the work involved in stripping out the relevant parts before the offending pump can be removed and a replacement installed can take an amateur around two days' work. However, a measure of the degree of bearing wear can be gained by grasping the pump hub and rocking it to test for play. Moreover, when the engine is started there should be no screech or rumble. Untold damage can be done to the pump bearing by running the fan belt too tightly in an effort to prevent slip. The belt need only be tight enough to ensure correct tension on the pulley; correctly adjusted, the bearing should give no trouble. The larger

A superb under-bonnet view of a Plus 2S. Anyone finding a car for sale in this condition would be lucky and doubtless the asking price would be equally impressive!

cars, of course, have electric fans so bearing wear is even less of a problem.

It goes without saying that the twin Weber carburettors are a great temptation for 'fiddlers'. Here again, though, when properly set up they should give many trouble-free miles. However, this is one area which is best left to the experts with their specialised adjusting tools. It is reckoned that adjustment of the Webers can either make or mar the engine's character; correctly set up the engine will run smoothly, delivering its correct power output, but badly adjusted, the engine feels rough and down on performance. Incidentally, the Webers are mounted on rubber O-rings which isolate the carbs themselves from the hot manifold in order to reduce fuel frothing in the float chambers. As a result, there should be a degree of free play between the engine and the carbs. If there is not, someone has been over-tightening the mounting bolts, so beware!

On start up the unit should turn over easily with no clanks or mechanical protests. If these do occur, the starter drive may be worn. The Lotus unit was never the quietest but anything more than a subdued ticking sound from the top end may indicate a worn tappet or camshaft lobe, while metallic noises from the bottom end which begin to diminish as

The condition of the interior is equally as important as the running gear and chassis. Retrimming by a professional is expensive although, with care, it is possible to make a good job yourself.

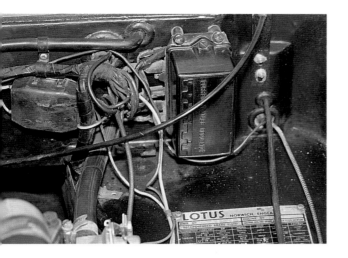

(Left) *Electrics can often be a nightmare, even to the proficient engineer. Modifications to the wiring using taped joints or signs of wires which have been damaged by overheating should be checked carefully.*

(Right) *Safety belts can often become worn over the years (despite being an MoT check) and help to make the car's interior look down-at-heel.*

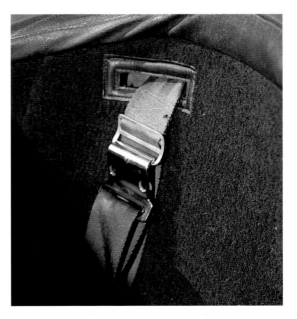

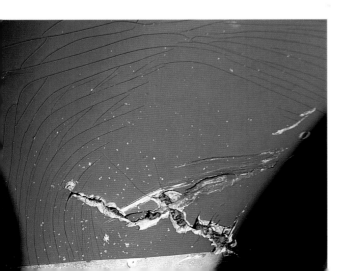

An example of body crazing. While the Elan's GRP body-shell is immune from rust this sort of damage needs careful attention to repair before painting.

the temperature increases could indicate worn crankshaft bearings. As the engine warms up there should be no obvious rattles; look at the degree of adjustment left on the timing chain tension screw on the left-hand side of the timing case. Little or no adjustment clearly indicates that a new chain will be needed soon. Once warm, oil pressure should be around 38–40psi and idle it should be as low as 20psi. However, clouds of smoke issuing from the exhaust when the engine is revved indicates a major engine rebuild.

Having convinced yourself that the engine starts happily (it is as well to start and then switch off a couple of times just to check the starter mechanism) the next step is a road test. Ideally, you should conduct at least part of this yourself since trying to judge wear and 'feel' while someone else is driving is almost impossible.

Under normal driving conditions, the oil pressure should behave as has been indicated; a wavering needle can suggest worn big or main bearings and even a worn oil pump. Under normal acceleration there may be a slight oil mist but nothing more. A blue haze illustrates worn valves or piston rings while if the same haze appears on over-run then it is quite likely that the valve guides are worn. The water temperature gauge should remain constant throughout the test. Any rise and fall which corresponds with engine speed may well indicate a blown head gasket; the water system is being pressurised by the increased engine temperature with a resultant loss of coolant.

Next to consider are the clutch and gearbox. The drivetrain of a sports car always takes a greater pounding than that of a saloon so look for baulking of the synchromesh as changes are made from gear to gear, especially into first on the move. The Ford gearbox is renowned for its longevity, but a hard life can have the unit jumping out of gear as the wear builds up. (The five-speed gearbox on the Plus 2S, however, is not so robust and should be tested for weak synchromesh.) Also, test for smoothness in the clutch action; there should be no traces of snatch as the clutch is engaged or slip as the throttle is opened.

When stepping into a Lotus there is always the urge to use the performance to the full; this is not necessary and does not help in trying to assess the car's condition. A lot can be learned about its faults by driving purposefully and carefully: does the car pull to one side when the brakes are applied? Does the steering self-centre properly? Are there any nasty crashing sounds as the suspension tries to cope with pot-holes?

When the road test is over, lift the bonnet once more to check if there are any water or oil leaks. Even if the engine has been freshly cleaned, a bad weep will show up after a reasonable run which has allowed the engine to get completely warm.

In contrast to the technics, the bodywork and interior are more the icing on the cake, the frills or cosmetics. But, nevertheless, these areas are equally important since they either make or ruin the car visually. Remember, too, that the last all-factory-made Plus 2Ss were pretty complex motor cars. A great deal can be learned about the car – the way it has been looked after and the owner's attitude – from the condition of the paintwork and the interior trim. It is just not good enough for an owner to say, 'Well, what do you expect for a car of this age?' when the trim is tatty or torn, especially if the asking price is in the top bracket. That said, many specialists agree that with the Elan/+2 construction technique, it must be assumed that there will be some cracking of the gel coat; a small price to pay, they reckon, for rust-free GRP bodywork. Like the chassis frames, it is possible to buy any body panel – including a whole new Elan shell – for these models, although a botched body repair not only looks horrid but, unless the job has been done properly to start with, there will be problems with surface deformity later.

Water leaks were a particular problem on early Elans so inspect for ingress and poor- or badly-fitting weather strips. Wear in the hinges can occur as time progresses, especially where electric window lifts are fitted. Also, remember that hoods and/or tonneau covers can be expensive to replace and that rips or tears will have allowed rain to get in leading to the possibility of rotted carpets or damaged trim panels. Inside, the seats and carpets can often reveal just how much of a hard life the car has had. It is now possible to buy complete carpet sets and seats can be retrimmed, so there is no excuse for a tatty interior.

However, very real problems can be encountered with the last of the +2s with their impressive dashboard layouts and numerous electrical extras. While many DIY enthusiasts pride themselves on their dexterity with a spanner, a car's electrics remain a mystery and a badly botched wiring loom can be a nightmare to put right. So look out for odd bits of wiring and spare lengths of insulating tape. An under-bonnet fire in a Lotus can be catastrophic!

Finally, try to be objective about the car. Make a total of what will have to be spent in an effort to rectify any problems and relate that to the asking price. It is sometimes possible to negotiate a good deal when the cost of replacing all the worn items has been taken into account.

BUYING: FOR RESTORATION

Of course, when it comes to seeking out a car which will form the basis for a restoration project things get much simpler. However, there is one golden rule which applies here: no matter how attractive the proposition, it really does make sense to buy a complete car. An owner may have dismantled the car in readiness for a full restoration programme only to lose interest or run out of money. But,

has he kept all the bits and are they all in clearly identifiable boxes? Such a car might seem cheap and an irresistible bargain but can very soon lose its appeal when it is discovered that some hard-to-find parts are missing or all the suspension mounting bolts have just been tossed into a box and jumbled up. Imagine the frustration!

As has already been said, the Elan is almost infinitely rebuildable, so a restoration should give few problems. There are many respected Lotus specialists about nowadays who can help with the work and supply the right parts. It is also possible to change the car to suit the individual. Just remember Albert Adams's words, though: the +2 was never designed to be made into a soft-top!

RUNNING TIPS

Since the Elan and +2 were designed to be assembled as kit cars and were produced by a smallish company which did not have the enormous facilities of the big manufacturers, their construction profile was much simpler than many other classic sports cars of the period. Parts are small, light and easy to handle and in general they can be dismantled easily for repair. Moreover, Elans were built in the days before the intricacies of engine management systems had become part of our everyday lives. So, although the power unit is reasonably highly-tuned, most maintenance jobs (though not all) can be tackled with confidence by the competent DIY owner.

Most Lotus experts agree that the only way to keep an Elan or +2 in top roadworthy condition is by constant preventative maintenance. Check, check and check again are the bywords for keeping the car in top reliable condition. This means planning an inspection programme which includes looking at the condition of all the vital points on the car on, say, a monthly or bi-monthly basis. Better that than to get stuck by the

An Elan Sprint body-shell which has been removed from its chassis, prepared and then sprayed. Attention to detail during the rubbing down process ensures a good finish later.

Door handles can become pitted with the passage of time. The best solution is a replacement.

When checking the condition of the body, inspect the wheelarches thoroughly since these are stress points and can become cracked and crazed.

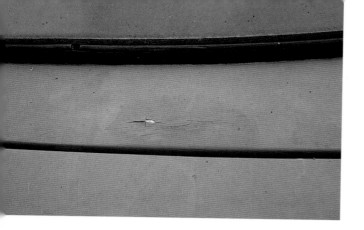

Another check point when looking at the condition of a car's body is the shut lines of the doors and boot. Worn door hinges can cause the doors — especially the heavier doors on the +2 — to drop badly.

The silencer system on a low-slung sports car like the Elan can easily become damaged. It is, of course, an MoT check point.

This rather sorry-looking +2 may well make a good foundation for a restoration project, although be prepared for the worst when looking at the chassis, suspension and drivetrain.

roadside during what was supposed to be a fun day out. This is just as important if the car is used only occasionally as if it is used as everyday transport.

One of the most important areas — and one often forgotten by the enthusiastic owner — is the electrical system. Because the Lotus uses a GRP body, each electrical gadget (including lights, wipers and so on) needs its own separate earth return. These should be kept clean and tightly connected if the system is to function properly. A good piece of advice here is to install a separate isolator switch. This should be let into the battery feed lead which, when operated, powers down the electrical system when the car is left. Perhaps it is also worth mentioning that it is wise to invest in a suitable fire extinguisher; better safe than sorry!

Next comes the body. While the Elan and +2 owner have the last laugh over the steel-bodied sports car fanatics, the bodywork still requires some attention to keep it looking smart. Regular washing prevents a build-up of road dirt (tiny particles can play havoc with the smooth GRP finish) and a good wax polish will maintain its sparkle. Inside the car, the vinyl coverings can be cleaned using warm water, while the trim panels can be treated to the occasional spray and polish using one of the aerosol cockpit cleaners now available. As previously mentioned, the Plus 2S was by far the most complex of the range being the most extensively equipped as well as boasting the most lavish interior. Allowed to become tatty and worn, these cars soon begin to lose their appeal. Incidentally, even during the summer months it is as well to operate the pop-up headlights occasionally to ensure they function correctly. If you find that the lights on the Plus 2 begin gradually to rise up from their resting place, this is a sure sign there is a vacuum problem. It is as well to lubricate the pivot spindles periodically to help prevent seizure.

Suspension-wise, the standard damper units are not the most long-lasting and if originality is not a consideration then dampers from, say, Koni will last much longer. As you are checking round the car feel for wear in the wheel bearings, wishbone bushes and suspension trunions. As with the checks involved with buying, regularly place the car on ramps so that you can get underneath to inspect the condition of the chassis and carefully clean out the mud traps. At the front, look at anything and everything for possible signs of wear or failure. Grip the starter motor and dynamo to see if their mounting bolts have worked loose, and talking of mountings, look to see how the exhaust system is lasting and the condition of its mounting points. Finally, cast an eye over the steering rack gaiters and the crankcase and sump for signs of oil leaks.

With the rear of the car in the air, the final drive can be checked, as well as the usual cleaning operation of the chassis frame. Pay some attention to the handbrake system, too. It goes without saying that this should be kept well lubricated in order to function properly. Talking of the braking system, this should be given a regular service which should at least include removing the pads. The calliper body should be given a thorough clean (especially where the pads are mounted), the discs checked and the pistons moved to ensure that they have not become seized. And do not forget those rubber drive-shaft doughnuts. Inspect for cracking and general deterioration. Opinions differ over the wisdom of fitting solid shafts with integral UJs, although clearly these units do transfer the stresses usually absorbed by the rubber driveshaft couplings directly to the differential mountings.

Under the bonnet, the radiator should be flushed through and filled with the recommended water/anti-freeze solution to ensure efficient operation of the cooling system. (The inhibitors help reduce the corrosive effects on the alloy cylinder head casting.) Always replace a hose which is beginning to show signs of cracking or which has become damaged through being covered in oil; better that than to lose all the coolant far from home!

Frequent oil changes ensure a healthy bearing life as well as keeping down sludge in the sump. But it is better to resist the temptation to fiddle with the carburettors unless the proper equipment setting-up is available or you are reasonably experienced. As has already been said, the carb settings can make or mar the running temperament of the car. If oil is beginning to escape from the cam box gaskets or the retaining studs, this can easily be remedied by fitting either a replacement gasket or using the proper washers under the retaining nuts. Finally, it is always better to keep the engine clean by giving it an occasional work-over with an engine cleaner; not only does it mean that you will stay clean when making quick inspections, it also adds to the look of the car — a car you will be proud to own.

LOTUS OWNERS ABROAD

For those Lotus owners overseas, running an Elan can have its fair share of nightmares, not least of which is being able to buy the right spares when they are needed. In a country like Canada, for example, Elan sales were limited when the car was new and, indeed, despite the company's best endeavours, the level of Lotus sales in the late 1980s has hardly rocketed. This means that it simply is not viable for an agent to deal specifically in Lotus sales and spares as demand just does not warrant it. Whoever takes on a Lotus franchise will also need to deal in at least one other car manufacturer's products.

Lotus ownership throughout Canada is very fragmented and owners will often drive hundreds of miles to attend a meeting. However, the pure logistics of running a vehicle such as an early Elan demands that its owner constantly keeps abreast of the car's servicing and general state of repair, which in turn means ordering spares in advance. It is nothing for an Elan owner in Canada to carry a small stock of spares to cover maintenance (and the usual failures due to the general ageing of the car) for the next twelve to eighteen months of motoring. In fact, this planned maintenance has an unlikely spin-off for foreign owners. Inevitably, it will mean coming into contact with other Lotus enthusiasts and specialists, both at home and in the UK. Much of the fun, then, in owning an Elan is in meeting people and making new friends.

For the less mechanically competent Canadian Elan owner, however, finding a suitable garage with an engineer skilled enough to work on a Lotus can be a problem. Like Americans, most Canadians look upon their cars as an 'appliance' and the majority of Canadian cars are nowhere near as intricate as a Lotus, even an early Elan. Colin Chapman's designs have often been compared to those of light aircraft. As such, they need a delicate approach. An alternative for the non-technically-minded owner is to redefine his or her abilities and, armed with a workshop manual, begin to teach themselves.

Running an Elan in a country where the climate is such that the temperature can plunge to −30°F (−34°C) can have some devastating effects on the car's technics and bodywork. For example, at these sorts of levels the GRP body can begin to crack. People who do drive in these conditions often keep their cars in a heated garage at home and put the car in another heated garage when they arrive at work. Moreover, it is essential that both the electrical and cooling systems are in the best possible condition.

In the States, the situation is very similar to that in Canada and Elan owners often need to drive long distances to their local Lotus specialist. Indeed, for many American owners the Elan is their second or even third car.

It's worth checking to see that the pop-up headlights really do pop up when they are supposed to.

Deterioration in the overall finish of a car will be shown up in areas like this around the windscreen. The best solution is a complete restoration replacing rusting screws with new ones.

This means that they can tolerate the 'funny little foreign car' if it goes wrong and is in the workshop for long periods. But, as in Canada, the American owner needs to choose a garage carefully and ensure that the staff are fully familiar with working on a Lotus.

Surprisingly, despite Lotus's reputation on the race tracks over the years, the company seems to have been less than aggressive in their efforts to sign up US dealerships for the purpose of selling their products. Some say that Lotus entirely misread the American market in the early days when the race cars were doing so well on tracks like Watkins Glenn. Even today, mention Lotus and the Ford connection to the average American enthusiast and the reply will be 'Oh yes, Lotus used Ford engines in the cars raced at Indianapolis' not, 'Oh yes, wasn't the Elan's engine based on a Ford unit?'

Like the Canadian owner, American Elan owners can face bodywork problems because of extreme climatic conditions, although in their case as a result of extreme heat as well as severe cold. And while the cooling system will probably work quite happily in average motoring conditions, an Elan in a hot summer's traffic jam will soon show its disapproval!

In complete contrast, the Elan has proved to be a popular sports car with the Japanese market, simply because in Japan it is considered to be a *real* sports car in sharp contrast to the sporting cars their own manufacturers produce. Despite the logistics of supplying parts to a market-place on the other side of the world, there are Lotus agents in Japan who are only too happy to supply the average owner with whatever is required to keep the car on the road. In addition, Japanese mechanics are more used to working on small, delicately tuned cars such as the Elan.

In view of the latest version of the Elan, this situation is likely to improve still further!

7 Maintaining the Breed

For the owner contemplating an Elan or Plus 2 restoration project there are a number of factors in his favour which must be the envy of many other classic sports car enthusiasts: Lotus owners are certainly well served when it comes to specialists and spares — not to mention the factory itself. The Elan (although less so the Plus 2) is straightforward and uncomplicated and most parts are easy to dismantle and the glass-fibre body is easily repairable with none of the problems associated with restoring metal bodies.

CHASSIS REPLACEMENT

The foundation for any Elan or Plus 2 restoration programme must begin with a sound chassis. And that means either sandblasting and repairing the existing one or, better still, throwing it away in favour of a genuine Lotus galvanised replacement. Since the average Elan is now twenty years old it must be expected that rust has taken its toll, particularly on the more vulnerable

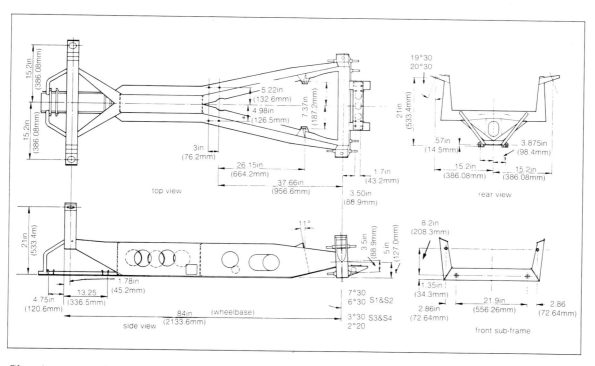

Chassis — general arrangement.

RAC/FIA HOMOLOGATION LIST

FIA REC' NO	LOTUS REF	VALID FROM	COMMENT	NOMENCLATURE
127	26/H/1	27.5.1963	Optional equipment	Heavy-duty suspension Rear anti-roll bar and alternative diameter front roll-bar Pin-drive, knock-on magnesium wheels, 5½in rim section, with hubs to suit 5.50 × 13 and 5.00 × 13 tyres 100-litre long-range fuel tank Hard-top 3-litre capacity alloy cross-flow radiator 6-litre capacity oil cooler
127	Elan 26/R	11.4.1964	Amendment	Maximum valve lift 10.42mm (0.41in) Outside front brake 228mm (9in) Long-range fuel tank is 52 litres, not 100 litres Alloy cross-flow radiator has separate header tank which gives a total water capacity of 8.5 litres
127	Elan 26/R	11.7.1964	Add to optional equipment Add to alternative final-drive ratios	Limited-slip differential Sump shield Light-alloy differential housing 3.444:1; number of teeth 9/31
127 B/V	26/H/1	16.11.1964	Add to options	Alternative magnesium wheels 6in rim width giving increase in track: front 1¼in, rear 1¼in
127 1/ET	26/H/1	1.2.1965	Variant to standard production from 26/3901	New dash panel facia & interior trim New rear light cluster Girling Type 14 front brake callipers KO pressed-steel disc wheels on all cars 125E connecting rods 1.50in (3.8cm) diameter EN52 inlet valves
127 C/V	26/H/1	1.2.1965	Add to optional equipment	Alternative heavy-duty rear suspension incorporating roller-spline driveshafts and Hardy Spicer universal joints to replace rubber Rotoflex couplings; 4.802in (12.197cm)/4.805in (12.205cm) centre to centre, EN19 connecting rods, weight 0.511 kg 2.530in (6.43cm) long × 1in (2.54cm) diameter gudgeon pin
127 D/V	26/H/1	1.8.1965	Add to optional equipment	1.562in diameter EN52 inlet valves Two 45 DCOE Weber (35, 36, 37, 38, 39, 40, 41mm) CW & P ratio 3.55:1; teeth 9/32
127 D/V	26/H/1	1.8.1965	Variant to standard production from 26/4518	Different carburettor gaskets with spacers & rubber 'O' rings

RAC/FIA HOMOLOGATION LIST

FIA REC' NO	LOTUS REF	VALID FROM	COMMENT	NOMENCLATURE
127 A/V	26/H/1	1.2.1966	Add to optional equipment (Group 4)	Dry-sump lubrication kit, part No. Cos/Mk 13/66 Forged steel crankshaft, part No. XVI 2001
527	—	1.2.1966	Optional equipment	Alternative CW & P and number of teeth: 4.4:1; (9/40), 4.1:1; (9/37), 3.7:1; (9/34), 4.7:1; (7/33), 3.55:1; (9/32) Hard-top. Ref. No. 26-B-730A
527 B/U	1	1.7.1966	Corrections to original forms	Convertible: Rear window — amend to plastic Wheel attachment — amend to knock-on Options: Interior heating system Dashboard-mounted radio Available in RHD and LHD versions
527 B/U	2	1.7.1966	Evolution changes	Modified silencer Modified top radiator hose arrangement Fabricated 4-branch exhaust manifold introduced
527 B/U	3	1.7.1966	Additional optional equipment	Servo-assisted brakes Steering lock integral with steering column
527	4	1.8.1966	Variant to standard production	New body style on all convertibles from chassis No. 45/5701
527	5	1.8.1966	Alternative body style	New coupe body style from chassis No. 36/4510; available in RHD and LHD versions
527	6	1.8.1966	Alternative body style — coupe	Weight — 1,527lb (692.65kg) Rear window — toughened glass
527	7	1.8.1966	Variant to standard production	From chassis No. 45/5701 (convertible) weight: 1,513lb (686.3kg) From chassis No. 36/4510 (coupe) & 45/5701 (convertible) sliding system for door windows — electrically operated vertical slide
527 B/U	8	1.7.1966	Evolution — Group 3	Continental knock-on wheels
527 D/V	9	1.11.1966	Variant to standard production Additional optional equipment	From 36/4510 & 45/5701: battery moved to boot From 36/4510 & 45/5701: Salisbury Powrlok limited-slip differential available
527	10	1.11.1968	Variant to standard production	From 36/7895 & 45/7896: all Elans fitted with new body style
527	11	1.11.1968	Variant to standard production	From 36/7895 & 45/7896: all Elans have revised interior

parts of the chassis frame. Even if it has already been repaired it is better to discard it unless it is in really good shape.

Removing the entire body from the chassis structure is, in fact, a job which can be tackled by a competent owner with sufficient space to be able to work in comfort and store the body while the new chassis is being built up. The saving in labour costs over having the job done by a professional is considerable. But, as was mentioned in the previous chapter, be prepared for the job to snowball once the car is stripped down. Paul Bing, long-time Lotus enthusiast, owner of one of the last Plus 2Ss made — now with over 130,000 miles (209,200km) on the clock — and Field Service Engineer for Lotus Cars, recommends that the best way to attempt this task is first to raise the whole car to a good working height, supporting the chassis on four sturdy axle stands. Thus, not only is it still possible to work easily under the bonnet in the engine bay, but there is also enough clearance to actually get under the car to

A detail shot showing an Elan rolling chassis. If the chassis structure has been affected by rot it should not be plated but replaced.

If properly maintained Elans can make good everyday cars.
This S4 model has clearly been kept in top condition.

attack things like the fuel line, exhaust system and reversing light switch.

First, disconnect the battery and remove it, storing it in a safe, dry place. Then, remove the starter motor cable between the starter itself and the solenoid and disconnect the leads connected to the dynamo. Next, drain the oil and water and disconnect the speedo drive from the speedo head mounted in the dashboard, carefully pulling the cable through the engine bulkhead and, using insulating tape, secure it safely to the engine so that it is out of harm's way. Now, move on to the brake and clutch systems removing the pipe between the manifold and the servo itself. Tie a label to it and store it away. Disconnect the clutch from the master

cylinder and the brake pipes from their master cylinder.

Next come the remainder of the engine controls and feeds to the instruments; the accelerator and choke cables to the carburettors, the water temperature gauge lead and the oil pressure gauge feed. Again, these should be taped to keep them safe while the body is being removed. Life will be made easier if the carbs are removed complete and stored away in a plastic bag, to be cleaned and overhauled later. Disconnect the braided earth lead on the coil as well as the high and low tension leads from the distributor. Pull off the heater hose from the water pump and secure this out of the way along with the second heater hose which locates with the water thermostat. Then, disconnect the headlamp vacuum feed pipe to the inlet manifold and the second headlamp vacuum pipe to the reservoir. You can now attack the steering column by releasing the retaining bolt at the rack end of the column.

Now turn your attention to the reversing light switch located on top of the gearbox and disconnect the wire to the rear light. Then, undo the inner seat belt anchorages which locate through to the chassis and remove the rear silencer. Carefully remove the petrol feed from the fuel tank and drain any excess petrol into a can and then screw the lid on tightly before storing it away safely. Remove the knob from the gear lever and disconnect the handbrake mechanism from the underside.

Back inside the car, remove the carpets, clean them and then store them away in plastic bags. This will then allow access to the sixteen body retaining bolts. These are located in the following positions as pairs, one on each side of the car: through the rack mounting pads locating with the front section of the body; from the radiator through the body to the front suspension turrets; through the side chassis flanges into the shell and behind the dashboard, through its support bracket to locate with the chassis frame below; from inside the cabin backwards to locate with the rear suspension turrets; and at the extreme rear of the car between the chassis and inside the boot.

'Now,' said Paul, 'it is possible to lift the body from the chassis either by using a proper body lifting jack (a pretty fierce-looking device used by specialists and the factory for removing bodies "the easy way") or by asking for the help of three friends.' Most people will have little choice but to use the second option, but ensure that people lift from beneath the sill sections and *not* from under the wheelarches because these are weak spots on the body.

Before starting to remove parts from the old chassis and overhauling them in readiness to fit them to the new one, drop the whole unit back on to its wheels once more and manoeuvre it into a position so that a small hydraulic or hand winch can be used to remove the engine and gearbox. This can then be placed either on the work-bench or pushed to the end of the garage and covered over to keep out moisture. Alternatively, the engine can be separated from the clutch housing and the engine then sent away to be overhauled by a specialist.

The chassis, now considerably lightened having shed its weighty power unit and gearbox, can be returned once more to its axle stands so that the real work can begin. Remove the suspension components and overhaul them thoroughly with new bushes and trunions. Perhaps even treat them to a coat of Hammerite before fitting them to the new chassis frame. Paul said that the best way to approach this task is to treat each corner of the car as a separate job and after stripping each unit down you must be careful to put all the bolts back so they are not confused or lost.

While the old chassis is still supported on its axle stands, the new chassis should either be supported in a similar fashion or placed on two very sturdy planks of wood, one under the front crossmember and the other under the differential housing. As with the old chassis, it should be placed at such a height that working on it is as comfortable as possible. It should be possible to fit the suspension struts with the dampers at full travel, still having some ground clearance left. Parts which have become covered in oil can be thoroughly cleaned using a degreasing agent, while rusty items can be either wire-brushed or even sand-blasted before painting. All brake pipes should be renewed using replacement flexible hosing between the suspension points and the chassis renewed with new copper tubing cut and shaped to fit and located onto the chassis itself. Ideally, the suspension struts should be replaced and the steering rack either

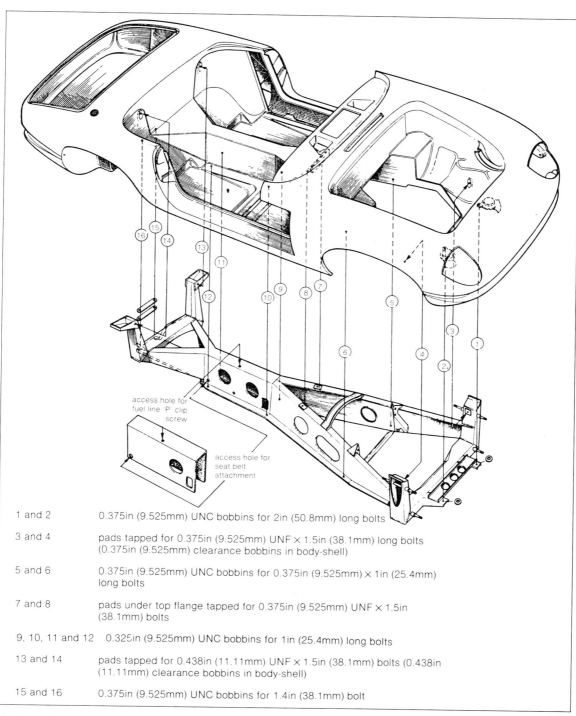

1 and 2	0.375in (9.525mm) UNC bobbins for 2in (50.8mm) long bolts
3 and 4	pads tapped for 0.375in (9.525mm) UNF × 1.5in (38.1mm) long bolts (0.375in (9.525mm) clearance bobbins in body-shell)
5 and 6	0.375in (9.525mm) UNC bobbins for 0.375in (9.525mm) × 1in (25.4mm) long bolts
7 and 8	pads under top flange tapped for 0.375in (9.525mm) UNF × 1.5in (38.1mm) bolts
9, 10, 11 and 12	0.325in (9.525mm) UNC bobbins for 1in (25.4mm) long bolts
13 and 14	pads tapped for 0.438in (11.11mm) UNF × 1.5in (38.1mm) bolts (0.438in (11.11mm) clearance bobbins in body-shell)
15 and 16	0.375in (9.525mm) UNC bobbins for 1.4in (38.1mm) bolt

Body to chassis attachment points.

An under-bonnet view of an Elan Sprint. The Weber
carburettors are a fiddler's paradise. Adjustment may well be
best left to an expert.

In contrast to engines fitted with
Weber carburettors, those using
Strombergs may well prove to be
easier for the DIY owner to adjust.

The engine bay of this +2 needs a lot
of work to bring it back to pristine
condition. The best solution is to
remove the engine from the car.

cleaned and fitted with new bushes and shims or replaced completely. Then, with the new chassis fully 'dressed' the wheels can be put back and the whole thing lowered to the ground and pushed out of the way while work begins on the engine.

FUNDAMENTAL REQUIREMENTS

Not surprisingly, before starting any major work on the Lotus engine it is advisable — indeed essential — to consider the following. While this section covers the stripping and rebuilding of the engine, space precludes it from being comprehensive and no one should even attempt this work without being armed with a Lotus workshop manual and a copy of one of the excellent books on the subject such as *Lotus Twin Cam Engine* by Miles Wilkins, published by Osprey in 1988.

First, think carefully about what tools and facilities you will require. These include: a sturdy work-bench which, ideally, should take up the full width of a single garage, complete with a reasonably-sized engineer's vice securely mounted on its surface; adequate storage space to accommodate parts as they are stripped off (two layers of 12in (30.5cm) deep shelves well mounted to the back wall of the garage are suitable for this), together with a good supply of large plastic bags for storing parts.

An early +2 ripe for restoration. Unless you are familiar with the Elan it is as well to join a club and try to pick up some useful tips on the main weaknesses of the model before going to look at possible cars to buy.

Next, think about your collection of tools. Here again, Wilkins gives a complete breakdown on what you will need in order to undertake the job professionally and successfully. Your approach to the task is always important: work cleanly. A good tip is to have a large (say, 18in (45.7cm) square by 6in (15.2cm) deep) metal container to one side. Using one of the proprietary cleaners, parts can be cleaned in this as they are stripped off. They can then be washed off in warm water, thoroughly dried and stored away while other work continues. Also, remember that the job will take as long as it takes — do not try to hurry things along or take short cuts. If you get it wrong it could mean hours of unnecessary work and many pounds wasted.

ENGINE PREPARATION

With the engine and gearbox out of the car as a complete unit, sit it somewhere convenient and begin to clean it working from the top down using Jizer, Gunk, or something similar and a 1in (2.5cm) wide old paint brush. To prevent water entering the inlet tracts of the cylinder head pack them with large cotton

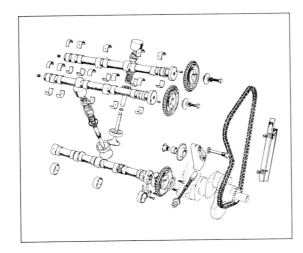

Valve gear components.

cloths which can be removed later. Work on one piece at a time, agitating the cleaner to remove stubborn grime. When you have finished, carefully rinse the piece off using a small sponge soaked in warm water. There may be some areas which will need a second application. Next, remove the clutch housing from the crankcase, then free the clutch housing from the gearbox. Thoroughly clean the inside of the clutch housing, dry it off, place the bolts you have just removed into a small bag and place them in the upturned housing which can now be stored away on a shelf.

If you drove the car before the restoration began you will have an idea of the condition of the gearbox. If it needs new bearings and synchromesh it is best to either send it away to a specialist or even — if it is badly worn — to replace it. Now, remove the starter and dynamo and dry them by placing them in front of a fan heater (or, perhaps, use a hairdryer) before storing them away (complete with their mounting bolts) in bags placed alongside the clutch housing. If the exhaust manifold has been left on, remove it and store it away too.

Of course, the ideal way to strip the engine is with the unit mounted on an engine stand. However, few people have one of these sitting in their garage, although you could, perhaps, fabricate one from angle iron. So, with the engine on the bench the strip-down format is as follows: cylinder head; clutch; flywheel; fuel and oil pumps; sump and front cover. This will then allow you free access to the main block assembly. Discard gaskets as you go and, while it is not absolutely necessary, remove the studs, too. Check machined surfaces which interface with gaskets for damage such as corrosion.

Begin by taking off the cam cover, gently easing it away from the cylinder head if it proves less than eager to budge. Remove the spark plugs and, unless they are almost new, throw them away. Then, with a socket on the flywheel nut, turn the engine until the notch

*A close-up of a show-prepared rolling chassis. Replacement of
the water pump is a long and involved job so fit a new one if the
engine has to come out for a rebuild.*

on the pulley is aligned with the TDC mark
on the front cover. Back off the timing chain
tensioner screw, remove the timing chain
sprockets and then release the camshaft
retaining bolts in correct rotation, carefully
marking both exhaust sprocket and cam
before inspecting the cams for scoring on
bearing surfaces and cam lobes. This done,
all four units can be stored away.

Next, remove the front plate/head bolts.
Then, with a torque wrench, release the head
bolts working in rotation, finally easing the
cylinder head away from the block. Inspect

for damage before placing it on a smooth
surface of the bench away from where you are
working on the engine. Continue to strip the
head, removing the valves – unless they are
in very good condition they should be
replaced along with all gaskets. Finally, give
it another clean, removing any remnants of
gasket before storing this away, too.

An Elan S4 drophead (overleaf). *The
best way to attempt a full restoration
programme is to take each step in a
logical fashion and not hurry the job.*

The Elan Sprint of 1973. Nowadays these are the most sought-after of the Elan range. A total restoration of these cars makes good economic sense.

Back at the block, undo the fan belt pulley bolt on the crankshaft and ease off the pulley along with the water pump pulley. Then, turn the engine around so that you have access to the flywheel, folding back the tab washers, removing the bolts and finally the flywheel. Next come the fuel pump, oil filter (obviously, this can be messy so be prepared with the large cleaning tray to hand) and finally, the distributor.

Next, turn the block upside down (again a messy business since the remainder of the oil and water will run out) and remove the sump and front plate cover. Either might prove a little troublesome, so carefully ease them free using screwdriver blades. Thoroughly clean out the sump and the front plate and store away.

You will now be able to get at the jackshaft drive and the oil pick-up pipe, both of which should be removed before making a start on the main and big end bearings, the crankshaft itself and the pistons. Remove the bolts from main bearings one and four and then two and three before releasing the bolts on the crankshaft bearing caps, finally pulling the crankshaft clear. Then, with the block rested on one side, the pistons and connecting rods can be pulled out through the top. All bearing housings (caps) should be carefully marked along with the connecting rods and pistons. Unless they are in exceptional condition, the bearings themselves should be thrown away. Finally, attend to the rear oil seal, the starter ring and the remainder of the water pump before the engine is reduced to its component parts.

It can be argued that assessing the degree of wear in engine parts is a matter of degree. However, a more positive approach is to take the crankshaft, cylinder block and pistons to Lotus agents for them to measure each unit properly. You can buy your new bearings and so on at the same time, since these are parts you *will* need. You can visually check the degree of wear on items such as sprockets as you reassemble the engine. Back with the cylinder head, it really is best to assume that (along with the valves) you will be fitting new springs and guides as well. As for the valve seats, before wasting time trying to lap in new valves, carefully inspect the seats themselves for cracks or corrosion. You will never get a gas tight seal with this sort of damage. Recut valve seats are the only solution and can be done at the same time as the valve guides by your local agent or machine shop.

Before beginning work on the head, check for any deformity by using a straight edge. If necessary, the cylinder head should be machined true. If all is well, clean away any build-up of sludge or carbon from the combustion chambers, getting rid of any dust using a compressed-air aerosol. Then, begin the reassembly work using the handbook and the excellent Wilkins book as your guide. Remember, it is one thing to strip the engine down but it is something else to put it back together using the manufacturer's tolerances so that it will run reliably again. Also, remember that cleanliness at all stages is very important, so clean each unit as it is put back. Take infinite care and delight in an almost surgical approach to the work – it will pay dividends.

In most cases the cylinder block will need a mild rebore at the very least, although if wear is minimal a slight hone (again, done by a specialist) will suffice to allow the new piston rings to bed in better. With the block back on the work-bench, work can begin to reinstall all its components. By this time the old pistons will have had new rings fitted (or the pistons themselves replaced) along with new small end bushes. Before starting the build-up proper, ensure that you have all the replacement parts – bearings, gaskets and so on – to hand. Also, invest in the latest, correct sealant, lubricating paste and non-hardening compound for use as the assembly job progresses.

ENGINE BUILD-UP

With the block inverted, insert new core plugs, oil gallery plugs and the drain plug tap or plug. Install new jackshaft bearings and lubricate them in readiness to take the shaft itself. Insert the new main bearing caps, installing the crankshaft *in situ* but leaving out the centre main bearing so that the endfloat can be checked. This will indicate the size of the thrust washers required. Finally, add the centre main bearing using a torque wrench to tighten the bolts, ensuring that the crankshaft turns freely as you go. Next, assemble the pistons with their gudgeon pins and bushes onto their respective connecting rods and begin feeding the rods carefully one by one into their respective bores. A ring clamp should be used to clamp the rings into place so that the pistons can be properly inserted without damage. With the correct pistons facing the right way in all four bores, the big end bearings can be fitted and lubricated, and the caps bolted into place and torqued down. Again, ensure the crankshaft turns freely.

Move on to the oil pipes before attempting to fit a new water pump assembly into the front plate. Heat should be used to expand the plate so that it will accept the new bearing. Remember, this job can take two days once the engine is back in place, so it is best to do it properly on the bench!

Turn now to the rear crankshaft oil seal, which is best fitted using hot water to expand the metal – do not forget to smear the seal-to-crankshaft surface with a little engine oil. You are now ready to fit the sump. Surprisingly, this is sometimes a fiddly job but, again, it is worth getting it right since a poorly seated sump pan will eventually allow oil to escape, causing a mess and a loss of expensive oil.

The clutch can be fitted next. Carefully align the plate with an aligning tool, making sure that the balance marks are set correctly, then replace the housing. Moving on to the front of the engine, the pulley wheel can now be added and the crankshaft turned so that the pistons are half-way down the bore. The complete unit can then be put to one side

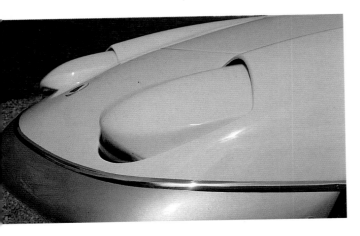

Failure of the pop-up headlights could be traced to a leak in the system. Later cars were fitted with a fail-safe design such that in such instances the lights will rise to their operating position.

An electric cooling fan with its thermostatically-controlled switch was standard equipment on the larger +2.

(cover it over if there are signs of dampness). The new valves can now be lapped in using a conventional lapping tool and engineer's blue to ensure that the two surfaces (the seat and gas seal surface of the valve) are mating correctly. Thoroughly clean away all paste before beginning assembly. Replace or renew the studs and then fit the valve rockers in their correct order before locating the camshafts in their positions – fitting new bearings of course. Ensure that the units rotate correctly and that there is no binding before finally fitting the timing chain sprockets. Shimming up the valves is an intricate operation too involved to cover here. Suffice it to say that this procedure cannot be hurried, so work carefully and methodically. Next, fit the entire head assembly onto the cylinder block, using two head bolts, at diagonally opposite ends of the engine to locate the gasket in its proper position before fitting the remaining bolts. Tighten the bolts to the correct torque setting then fit the timing cover and torque this into place ensuring a good gasket fit between the front plate and the cylinder head gasket.

The next job is to time the engine by fitting the timing chain with the sprockets correctly aligned. First, rotate the engine so that the TDC mark lines up with the front cover marks. Then rotate the camshaft sprockets so that their marks are pointing towards each other horizontally in line with the top of the cylinder head. Next, remove the camshaft sprockets and pull the chain up, feeding it over the exhaust sprocket first (bolting the sprocket to the camshaft) and finish with the inlet sprocket when it, too, can be bolted to its camshaft. Fit the tensioner mechanism and adjust it so that the chain is set to the requisite degree of free play.

At this point you may wish to paint the engine before fitting the fuel pump, dynamo and starter (together with their brackets), and the fan belt. When these are fitted, move the engine so that it aligns with the 10° BTDC mark and install the distributor, having first checked its vertical free-play movement. It is worth checking the timing once more at this stage to ensure that the camshafts and distributor really are in alignment! There is not much left now other than to fit the distributor cap, plugs and leads and then install the carburettors – with new gaskets, naturally. It is often forgotten just how worn carburettors can become over the years, so you may wish (at this point) to overhaul them or have them done professionally.

So, there you have it — the foregoing was simply intended to give a thumbnail sketch of what is involved, the keywords being *care* and *cleanliness* at all times.

When it comes to the body of the Elan or Plus 2, clearly the major benefit here is that, despite the car's external condition, there will be no trace of rust. It is still possible to buy body sections which can be laminated into place to repair either accident damage or to repair areas which have badly deteriorated through age. It is best to work on the body with the doors, bonnet and boot lid in place. With the chassis and suspension built up, as has already been discussed, and the drivetrain once more back in place, the body can be offered up to the chassis so, given that a new chassis frame has been substituted, the locating holes can be scribed onto the virgin chassis. The body must then be removed so that the locating holes can be drilled in readiness to take the locating bolts. Then, fit the body back on the chassis, remembering to locate a saddle of sound-proofing material between the centre section of the chassis and the body. The bolts can now be fitted and the two units — chassis and body — bolted together.

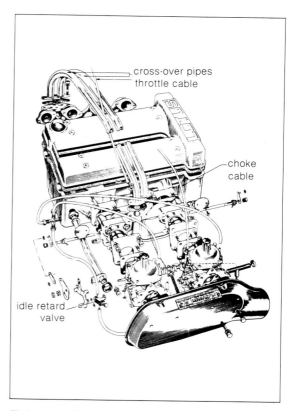

Exhaust emission system (Zenith Stromberg).

The single exhaust pipe of the later Elans was considered to be the best, giving quiet yet efficient performance.

The tool kit of an Elan Sprint.

THE FINAL FURLONG

Now that your pride and joy looks like a car once more, you can turn your attention to improving the look of the outside. But first, a word of warning because working with fibreglass, paint and thinners can be a dangerous business if you are careless. The best approach is to make it a golden rule never to smoke in the workshop. When working with GRP always wear goggles particularly if you are using a grinding machine or an orbital sander. Also, wear a face mask; tiny GRP particles are very bad for the eyes and lungs. If you happen to get a splash of hardener in your eyes wash them thoroughly with clean water and call the doctor. The GRP strands can be an irritant to the skin so it is also always best to wear protective gloves. Finally, always ensure that there is adequate ventilation in your garage or, better still, work in the open air. Should there be a fire when you are spraying, never treat it with water; either use a blanket or, better still, a proper fire extinguisher which should always be on hand to cope with such an emergency. Apply the same degree of cleanliness to the restoration of the body as was applied to the rebuild process of the engine. Never leave old tins or rags soaked in paint or thinners around the workshop.

Unfortunately, the best and indeed the only way to get a good finish on the GRP body is to remove all the existing paint from the shell. This will mean using a water-soluble paint stripper and working on small areas at a time, thoroughly washing off the stripper solution as you go. Finally, use 220 wet-and-dry paper, flat down the whole of the shell. Where the surface has been damaged by small holes, scratches or cracks these should be repaired. Scratches and pin-prick holes can be treated easily using filler and hardener. Serious stress cracks must be rectified with a more radical approach consisting of two layers: 1oz (28g) of matting applied behind the cracked area with resin

Clearly, the larger Elan +2 and Plus 2S models are more complex cars to restore and maintain. Lotus do not advise conversion of models into dropheads since the chassis/body design does not lend itself to this modification.

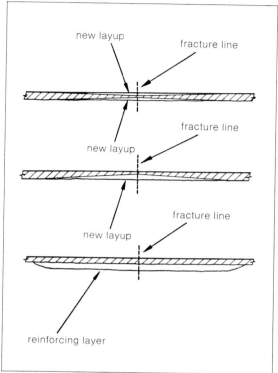

Basic bonds and joints.

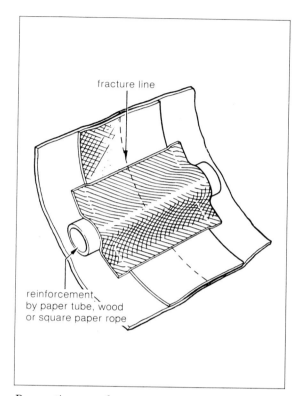

Box section over fracture.

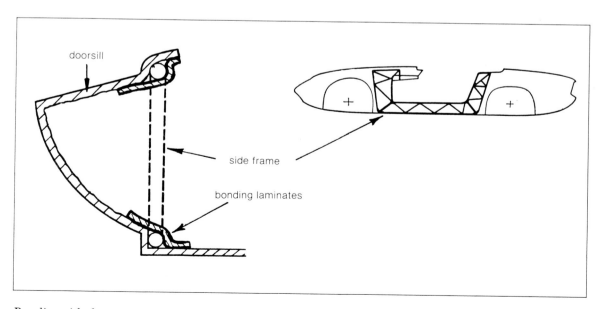

Bonding side frames.

The neat leather rim steering wheel fitted to a S4 drophead. Rings can sometimes damage the surface of the leather over a period of time.

The facia panel of a drophead Elan can become cracked and crazed from exposure to the weather. This will mean rubbing down the surface and revarnishing.

and fine tissue used above and covered by a veneer of filler to restore the bodywork contours. More serious body panel problems can be treated in the same way.

When a whole new body section is to be added, it should first be aligned with the existing shell using clamps to hold it in position. Care should be exercised to ensure that the new section is exactly in place. Then, the underside of both the old and new panels should be cut away in a shallow 'V' formation along the join line and the joint laminated together. Next, the top side should also be cut away in a similar fashion to form a shallow 'V', such that the new lamination beneath shows through along the line of the join. This is then laminated in readiness to be rubbed down. Use 220 wet-and-dry to start and follow with 320 grade to prepare the whole shell. As a yardstick to how long this work takes, even a professional will spend up to 100 hours on filling, preparing and flatting!

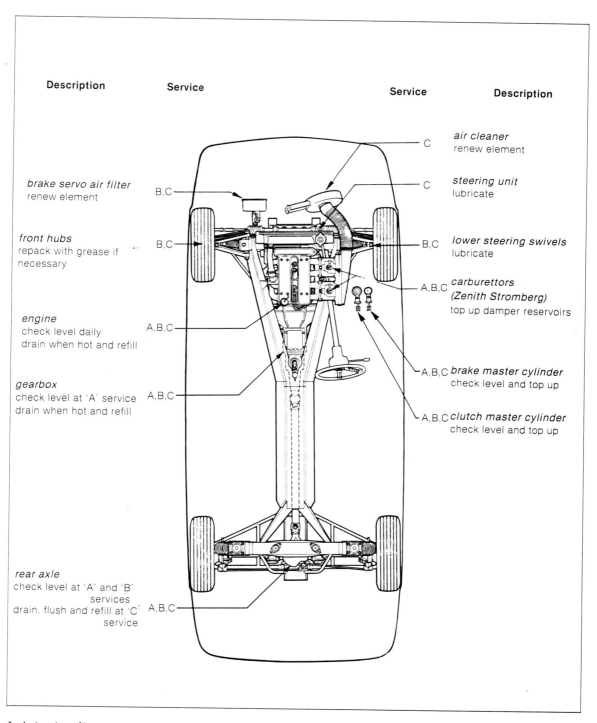

Description	Service		Service	Description

air cleaner
renew element — C

brake servo air filter
renew element — B,C

steering unit
lubricate — C

front hubs
repack with grease if
necessary — B,C

lower steering swivels
lubricate — B,C

carburettors
(Zenith Stromberg)
top up damper reservoirs — A,B,C

engine
check level daily
drain when hot and refill — A,B,C

brake master cylinder
check level and top up — A,B,C

gearbox
check level at 'A' service
drain when hot and refill — A,B,C

clutch master cylinder
check level and top up — A,B,C

rear axle
check level at 'A' and 'B'
services
drain, flush and refill at 'C'
service — A,B,C

Lubrication diagram.

A point to bear in mind is that any imperfections in your preparation work will show through after the paint has been applied!

Of the three types of paint available — acrylic, lacquer or cellulose — the favourite with the professionals is acrylic as the other two have a tendency to fade. With the body masked (although it is better to remove all chrome trim and glass) first spray on a coat of filler and follow this with a dark 'guide' coat which is then flatted down using 220 wet-and-dry paper. This will identify any areas which need further treatment. Follow with a second guide coat, again flatted down, and finally a covering of primer/sealer. This should be flatted down with 600 grade paper before two coats of primer are applied, each coat being flatted down with 600 grade as you go. The shortfall of using cellulose is that it requires a lot of thinners which can have an adverse effect on the carefully applied undercoats. Acrylic, however, can be applied in just one coat and in around seventy degrees Fahrenheit (twenty degrees Celsius)

will dry in three to six hours. However, it should be left for two weeks until it is really hard and able to withstand the rigours of polishing.

Retrimming the interior is a job which can be quite easily handled by the DIY owner. Although the seats are, perhaps, best left to a professional upholsterer, door and rear trim panels can easily be removed and recovered. Nowadays, it is possible to buy complete new carpet sets for both the Elan and the Plus 2. Throughout their production run both Elan model ranges were sent out to sub-contractors for this work, so trying to recreate originality is a little tough! The dashboards of the later Plus 2S models were comprehensive, although it is possible to remove all the instruments and controls before taking it out of the car to give it a repolish. A word of warning, though: carefully mark each and every wire as you pull it off a switch or instrument as trying to identify leads when it is time to put the dashboard back together can be a nightmare! Again, the watch-word is to work cleanly and not to rush things.

8 Horses for Courses

Not surprisingly, the Elan's pedigree makes it an ideal car for amateur competition use, and in good shape it should need very little in the way of modification to make it at least as good as the opposition in the Beginners Series. Indeed, in standard trim Elans should be capable of out-performing many of the supposedly dramatic machines to be found in club competitions. They really are 'horses for courses'. (The Plus 2S is less suitable, however, because – despite its wider track – it is bulkier and less nimble.)

A man with many years of experience with Elans – and a successful Elan campaigner – is Pat Thomas who runs Kelvedon Motors in Spalding, Lincolnshire. This firm can supply almost any part for a modified Elan. To anyone considering embarking on the competition trail, Pat offered the following advice:

'The first thing to look at is the commitment you will have to apply in order to go racing. If you start at the beginning of the season your first race will be in late March which will mean preparing the car during the depths of

Lotus began in business making sports/racing cars for the club-man competitor who raced at the weekend. Here is a typical example; an MG-powered Lotus Mark VI seen here at Castle Combe in 1954.

Anyone thinking of going racing with an Elan in the Road Sport Series is already one step ahead of people using other cars since the Elan's design has so much racing knowledge built into it.

*The Lotus Elite was really a road-going sports racer. One of the
earliest and certainly one of the most successful Elite
campaigners was Graham Warner in 'LOV 1' seen here at
Silverstone in 1961.*

winter. Imagine lying on the floor in an unheated garage.' He shuddered. 'I cannot stress strongly enough the degree of commitment that's required.

'To go racing – especially with the intention of doing well – you have to eat, sleep and breathe it' Pat continued. 'That said, no matter where you find yourself in the field, there'll always be someone else to race against so you can have just as much fun in mid-field as you can dicing for the lead.

'The start of the Sunday race really begins early on the Friday morning,' explained Pat, 'because nowadays so many of the meetings are two-day events which means arriving either late on Friday or early on Saturday to prepare for practice. Then, there'll be a lot of waiting around until the race itself which, as often as not, will not be until four o'clock on Sunday afternoon. Then, the car – or the bits if you weren't so lucky – has to be loaded back onto the trailer for the long drive home. If you're going to do well, you have to be at the first race and the last race in the season, not just the ones in the middle of summer when everyone's out sunbathing' recommended Pat. 'The key is to go out and do well at the beginning of the season when everyone else is still waking up. For someone who goes racing regularly his weekends will start on Friday mornings and end late on Monday evenings, thereby reducing his working week to just three days.'

RACING: AN INTRODUCTION

Pat Thomas is adamant that for the person new to racing it really is very beneficial to spend a season visiting the individual tracks and talking to the drivers and their teams. Clearly, no one is going to give away their hard-won experience, but many people like talking about their successes and the factors along the way that have contributed to that success. Subtlety is the key. To anyone fresh to competitive motor sport, Pat said he would suggest that the best introduction is either to sprint or hillclimb the car. The Elan is ideally suited to either of these events and the newcomer will soon learn how to move the car off the line quickly – and derive considerable pleasure from competing – without subjecting the car to the tremendous stresses that, say, even three laps of Silverstone's club circuit can impose. 'In three laps the discs can be glowing cherry red, the brake fluid can have boiled and the slave cylinder rubbers can have caught fire' explained Pat ruefully.

Pat said that another bonus for the novice Elan owner who decides on sprinting as an introduction to motor sport is that the car can be left totally standard. With the exception of the usual safety requirements (including, of course, a roll cage, fire extinguisher and protective clothing) and a set of adjustable dampers all round, the degree of financial expenditure will be well within the pocket of most enthusiastic beginners.

'I do maintain that it is the worst kind of false economy to be miserly over safety features' said Pat with feeling. 'Buy the best crash hat you can afford. After all, you only get one chance and even if the car is little different from standard, you can still kill yourself. In fact, it is probably easier to kill yourself in a road car than in a race car because the race car has been *designed* to go fast and handle properly at high speeds.'

As for hillclimbing, Pat said that it can be just as much fun as sprinting, with an equally small degree of stress on the car for short periods. He does, however, warn that it is probably easier for the novice to 'bend' his pride and joy because on certain circuits the tracks are very narrow with trees and ditches. But, if it is the race track where you are intent on competing, the next consideration is the condition of the car and – equally importantly – your own driving ability. Pat Thomas cautions:

'Remember that Elans are now around twenty years old. This means that the suspension components – uprights, wishbones and so on – have been subjected to all the usual forces (bumping up and down kerbs and so on) that any twenty-year-old car has been subjected to. Now, those very same suspension components will be asked to withstand even greater stresses imposed by the addition of racing tyres (which have a far greater adhesion quality than that of the tyres which were around when the Elan was new) and considerably greater cornering speeds!

'One sobering lesson which is very quickly learnt during the first time out is how slow you are compared to the others in the race – despite any preconceived notions of driving like a demon on the road' Pat laughed. 'I recall my introduction to club racing. It was at Silverstone and I'd got off to a good start. But, as I approached the first corner, I braked at the point I thought was right to get me round the corner and soon realised it was far too early. Everyone zoomed past me and I had to accelerate again to the right braking point, by which time everyone else had disappeared into the distance.

'Another point to remember,' advised Pat, 'is that you're not the only novice on the track trying to drive a car which clearly has a mind of its own. There'll be perhaps thirty other competitors out there, each trying to run you over in order to get in front. I've always

An Elan in the Prodsports DMB Motor Championship in 1977.

The Series 4 drophead, sleek and aerodynamic.

Surprisingly, if you are thinking of tuning the engine to produce more than 150bhp it is recommended that the chassis be changed to a spaceframe-type structure like those marketed by Spyder Engineering.

The Lotus engine — producing excellent racing power.

maintained that a fully sorted race car is far easier to drive quickly and safely than a road car. That said, the real magic of a Lotus — and the Elan in particular — is that it's so "user friendly". It is this which has kept me fascinated with Lotus cars over the years. It's almost as though Colin Chapman is sitting in the back and redefining suspension design as you go round a corner.'

When preparing the car it is advisable to go to someone like Pat Thomas who specialises in Elans and has experience with them. This could save the beginner a great deal of trial, error and heartache when it comes to arriving at a reasonable set-up for the car. Although there will always be those people who want to tackle their own development work, in general this approach will usually cost the individual more money.

RACING: GETTING STARTED

A popular competition starting point for the novice, especially one with a limited budget, is the Road Sports Series which is designed specifically for cars entered in standard form with only limited alterations (such as adjustable dampers) allowed. The springs, however, must *not* be altered and the engine should be prepared to the manufacturer's original specification. Next comes the Improved Road Sports Series which allows more radical modifications while still retaining the basic concept of the car. In this series the rules prevent the use of a highly modified body-shell or the addition of spoilers. However, it is possible to think in terms of bigger brake callipers with a balance-bar braking system to feed them and uprated springs to go with the adjustable dampers. The engine can be vastly improved to increase its horsepower (say, 170bhp or even more), although dry-sumping is not allowed.

As for wheel sizes for the Improved Road Series, Pat said that he would estimate that the average entrant would fit 6in wide wheels on the front and 7in wide on the rear. This is because the Elan's suspension is inherently softly sprung with a marked degree of camber change throughout its travel. However, the latest design in racing tyres is based on square section technology so the Elan will not be at its best with very wide wheels and tyres. 'The biggest mistake the novice often makes is fitting very wide wheels and setting up the suspension with oodles of negative camber because that's the way it worked with beam axles,' said Pat.

When it comes to engine preparation, Pat said that the Elan starts off with an in-built advantage over other cars. That said, the modifications will need to include a change of camshafts, a cylinder head with larger valves and replacement jets for the carburettors. Pat is a great believer in the adage that the most effective modification is often the cheapest. He is also firmly convinced that careful preparation pays dividends. 'For example, it is worthwhile fitting a well-baffled sump,' advised Pat, 'because this considerably reduces oil surge. If you don't, the likelihood is that you'll ruin the bearings first time out.'

As has already been said, even in standard form – albeit in first-class mechanical condition – the Elan is a very competitive car which needs little in the way of alterations or additions to give it an edge over others on the race track. Over the years a good many drivers have shown just how quick the Elan can be made to perform, the yardstick here being, of course, that the majority of the other cars on the circuit will be the products of a mass-production manufacturer so their chassis/onocoque/suspension design will not have had the enormous benefit of Chapman and his talented team behind them. However, in the modified classes, even the Elans bear only a passing similarity to a road car – and then only where the regulations require it. Clearly, these cars are very specialised and cost a great deal of money to build since so many of the components will be unique to racing cars. In these categories most entrants have sponsorships to offset the tremendous investment involved in building and running such a car; an investment, incidentally, which is continuous because in addition to the usual running and repair costs it will

also be necessary to maintain an ongoing development programme to keep the car competitive.

RACING: MODIFICATIONS FOR THE TRACK

Significantly, despite the much-praised backbone chassis design of the Elan and Plus 2, it is recommended that owners of cars with engines producing in excess of 150bhp think in terms of changing to a spaceframe chassis of the type marketed by Spyder Engineering of Peterborough. The beauty of this structure is that, not only is it easy to repair (struts can be cut out and new ones welded in their place), it is also stronger than the type originally fitted to the Elan. In addition, thought has gone into the question of accessibility for servicing so that the prop shaft, clutch slave cylinder, speedo drive and exhaust system are much easier to get at for maintenance. Areas which were particularly prone to stress cracks on the Lotus chassis have been strengthened, especially around the engine mounting points and the walls of the front suspension turrets, and blanking plates have been added to prevent road dirt from getting inside where it can create rust problems. Other thoughtful details include a removable crossmember (which allows the sump pan to be taken off while the engine is still *in situ*) and the fact that the front suspension is easily detachable. Having fitted uprated dampers it is now important to consider fitting uprated springs since the spring rates fitted on road-going Elans are specially chosen to give the car its high-quality ride. That said, they are too soft for serious competition work and someone like Kelvedon Motors can supply uprated versions 'off the shelf'.

While solid driveshafts are frowned upon by people who strive for originality, it is true that these units do eliminate wind-up in the rubber doughnuts which can be a weakness

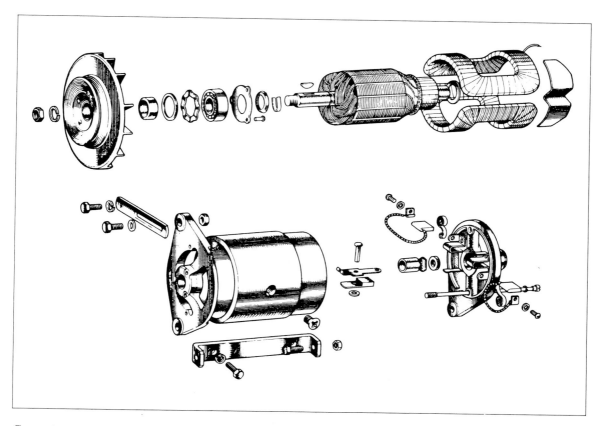

Generator components.

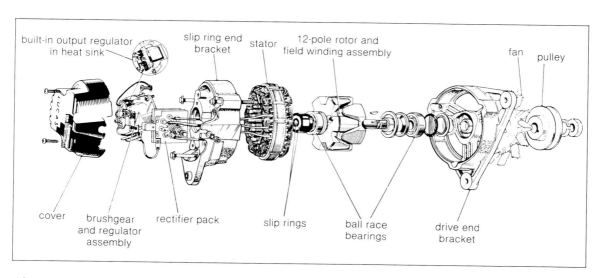

Alternator components.

Racing can put a great strain on suspension components such as wheel bearings and wishbone joints, especially when wide wheels and racing tyres are used.

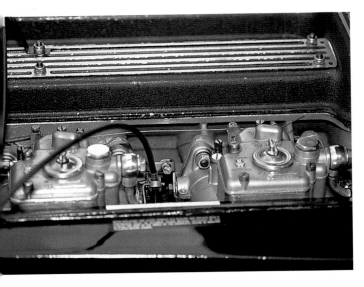

The 'Big Valve' engine.

under race conditions. However, in addition to reducing sponginess in the drivetrain, these units also provide crisper gear changes and the extra strain placed on the differential and its mounting points is reckoned to be an acceptable risk in this application. Again, Spyder Engineering, with their considerable experience in developing and marketing components for the Lotus range, offer two types of driveshaft: a solid version with sliding splines and universal joints; and one with universal joints at one end and special rubber doughnuts on the inner end. These couplings are so designed to react when power is applied so that surge is reduced and there is also a safety device to offset the possibility of a driveshaft shearing free from the coupling and doing untold damage to the chassis and body of the car.

Spyder also market a range of tubular wishbones for both the back and front suspension on the Elan and Plus 2. They are corrosion-resistant and lighter and stronger than the originals. Moreover, in true racing style they can be ordered with adjustable steel ball joints to enable the suspension to be set up to individual preference. Braking efficiency can be increased by fitting the standard Plus 2 brakes to the Elan and there are various ways of modifying the balance of braking performance between the front and rear callipers by using different pad material, pad size and limiting valves.

For extra performance – but without the need to increase the engine's capacity – the three areas to be considered are: cylinder head; camshafts; and carburettor jets and choke sizes. Hand-in-glove with this, of course, will be an improved exhaust manifold. An example of such a package was offered by Ian Walker Racing during the 1960s which was reckoned to produce 138bhp at 6,500rpm for a road-going Elan. The crankshaft, connecting rods and flywheel were dynamically balanced. High lift camshafts were fitted and the cylinder head was improved by polishing the ports and combustion chambers and increasing the compression ratio from 9.5:1 to 11:1. Other improvements included a stronger timing chain tensioner and a bigger oil pump feeding stronger crankshaft bearings.

As discussed in previous pages, cylinder blocks for Lotus were specially selected so that only those with thicker cylinder walls were used as the foundation for the 1,558cc engine. Most blocks will still have sufficient wall thickness to accommodate further boring to 83.5mm, producing an engine size of 1,594cc or even 85mm giving 1,650cc. The beauty of these 'basic' engine size increases is that the standard crankshaft and connecting rods can be retained without fear of failure. However, if a Lotus cylinder block is not available the best choice as a basis for building up a race engine is the 1,500cc Ford Cortina block which was used from October 1966 until the introduction of the taller 1,600cc 'Kent' engine the year after. While the production run of these blocks was clearly short, in this application they have the bonus of featuring thick cylinder walls, a six-bolt flywheel, square main bearing caps and a screw-in type oil pick-up connection. Unfortunately, the larger 1,600cc 'Kent' blocks were not interchangeable and would involve using a longer timing chain, the installation of a spacer for the timing chain cover and modification of the timing chain tensioner as part of a build-up.

The next step up from the 1,650cc unit is the 1,700cc engine. This would involve boring the block to 83.5mm and fitting a Cortina 1600 GT crankshaft, together with special connecting rods, thereby neatly overcoming the need to use cylinder block liners. Incidentally, the reason for specifying the GT crankshaft and not the shaft from the less powerful engine is that this has larger crankshaft counterbalance weights. Clearly, the higher the crankshaft speed, the greater the need for consideration of crankshaft balancing and counterbalance weights. By using the 1600 GT crankshaft and boring to

A novel photograph showing the inlet tract of an Elan cylinder head. Modifying a cylinder head is an expert's job and is very time-consuming; it is worth buying the best.

An Elan cylinder head. A gas-flowed head with larger valves should be accompanied by high-lift camshafts and rejetted carburettors to give maximum benefit.

85mm the engine size will be increased to 1,760cc, again without the need to resort to liners. If liners are considered, it is possible to increase the bore size to 86.75mm which will produce an engine size of 1,792cc, although the bore/stroke ratio will impose great strain on the crankshaft and bearings, particularly if standard components are to be fitted. Indeed, thought should be given, especially when producing these larger engine sizes, to subjecting the crankshaft and rods to one of the toughening processes like tuftriding or nitriding, together with the competition bearings. Another consideration when liners are to be used is the enormous cost of special pistons to fit non-standard bore sizes. The bonus of keeping with standard bore configurations is that only the con rods will have to be changed thereby keeping costs within reasonable boundaries.

The cylinder head can be modified to provide considerable increases in power; the inlet valves can be increased to 1.375in (34.93mm) and the exhaust to 1.25in (31.75mm) with suitable matching, polishing and machining as well. Clearly, the higher the compression ratio the greater the strain on the crankshaft and its bearings. (Since the 1,500cc Ford engine is an 'over-square' unit in its basic form, overboring it in the way just described puts even greater stresses on the bottom end.)

For the engine tuner there is a confusingly large range of performance camshafts from which to choose. Selecting the right one for your engine can be a nightmare and needs careful study of the manufacturer's claims and figures. Needless to say, it is a fruitless exercise to buy a camshaft which is not in keeping with the stage and capacity of the engine to be built. Too wild and there will be little useable torque in the low and middle rev ranges; too mild and the camshaft will not be able to take advantage of the characteristic of the cylinder head and the engine will run out of power too low down. Also, it is as well to check the manufacturer's recommendations over installation as the camshaft profile may well call for some other modifications to the engine.

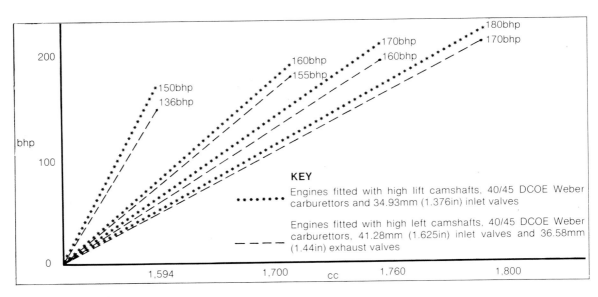

Brake horsepower against engine size for different engine fittings.

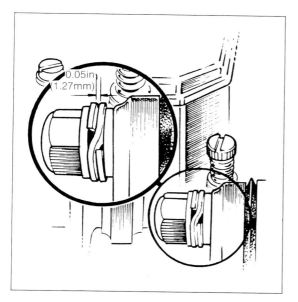

Double coil spring washer clearance (Weber).

Carburettor flexible mounting (Weber).

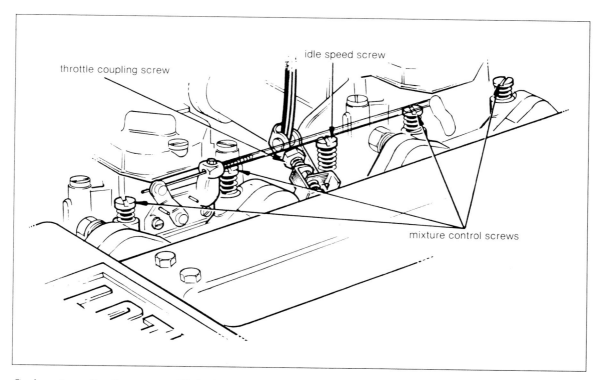

Carburettor adjusting screws (Weber).

The Elan engine starts off with a built-in advantage over other cars although if money is no object the unit can be modified to produce 170bhp or more.

Fuel injection is not considered to be of real value since the excellent Webers give almost the same performance. However, a good electronic ignition system producing a large spark is advantageous together with an oil cooler to reduce oil (engine) temperatures. A high performance clutch capable of handling the increase in power is mandatory, although the trusty Ford 2000E gearbox is rugged and should be capable of handling the additional power. For the higher-tuned engines, though, it would be worthwhile thinking in terms of having needle roller bearings fitted. Suffice it to say, there are a number of final drive ratios available to suit the car's state of tune and the characteristics of the circuit.

As with restoration work, the key to preparing a car for racing − particularly the drivetrain − is attention to detail. The people whose engines last a season without major maintenance are the people whose engines are built with care. Without care, the engine will be unreliable and will be forever needing to come out of the car for repairs.

For those who wish to modify their cars beyond the limitations imposed by the Improved Road Sports Series there is the Modified Sports Cars (or Modsports) Series in which the opportunities for development are almost limitless. Indeed, the main constraint on cars entered in these events would seem to be the size of the owner's bank account! This really is an area of racing for the person who wishes to use initiative in the car's development. 'The only rules here are that the car has to look like a sports car with the engine in the same place as when the car left the factory,' said Pat.

In this series the chassis, suspension, drivetrain and body can be as extreme and advanced as the builder wishes to go. Starting with the chassis, the wisdom of changing to a spaceframe-type chassis such as the excellent structures marketed by Spyder Engineering has already been discussed. This will provide a stronger, lighter framework upon which to base the racer and one that has been designed specifically with competition in mind. As mentioned, Spyder also offer a whole range of suspension items such as roll bars and wishbones with rose joints to allow the car to be set up specially for the individual driver. Moreover, this design of chassis is ideally suited to the addition of any extra stiffening which the builder may wish to include around the suspension, engine and differential mounting points. Clearly, at this level of competition rubber driveshaft couplings will have to be changed for solid units with universal joints capable of handling the torque being transmitted through the drivetrain.

Engine-wise, the regulations in this series leave the way open for limitless development using all manner of special racing components. In addition to the modifications already discussed for the Improved Road Sports Series, the use of steel crankshafts, specially made connecting rods and pistons can cost a small fortune − to say nothing of a high performance cylinder head. At this level of racing it is generally agreed that the engine used should be built up by a professional engine expert as there are a confusingly large number of tuning parts available for the tohc engine. The wrong permutation of camshafts, cylinder head and carburation could not only produce a lot less power than was expected but also at a considerable cost. At least an engine developed by a respected tuner should come with a dynomometer graph indicating both power and torque figures. Equally, the

gearbox should be fitted with needle roller bearings driving a Salisbury limited slip differential.

One of the most spectacular Elans ever built was Dave Brodie's 2.1-litre monster which he campaigned to good effect in Modsports. While the interior was very civilised for a Modsports racer, a glance at photographs of this car indicates the extreme alterations which had to be made to the body to take the ultra-wide wheels which were necessary to handle the performance. A brute if ever there was!

9 Return of the Elan

By any yardstick, the expansion of Lotus during those heady, frantic days of the late 1950s and early 1960s was impressive. Within a short time, their modest single-storey production area of 151,000sq ft (14,030sq m) and 26,000sq ft (2,400sq m) of office space at Hethel had more than doubled in size. Production methods had improved and an effort made to better the quality control, while Graham Arnold's PR exploits − if a little novel − certainly gave the motoring magazines much-needed Lotus news. The Lotus Cortina aside (from 1967 all Lotus Cortina production was handled in-house by Ford themselves, the name being subtly changed to Cortina Lotus!), by 1968 Lotus's model line-up included the fixed- and soft-top versions of the Elan, the bigger, more exclusive Plus 2 (for the family executive) and the two-door, fixed-hard-top, mid-engined Europa.

On the business side, Chapman was urged by his commercial advisor and friend, Peter Kirwan-Taylor, to float the company on the Stock Exchange and in 1968 Group Lotus Car Companies Limited was formed which encompassed Lotus Cars who were responsible for the manufacture of the road cars. Assembly-wise, the best year by far during this period was 1969 when some 4,506 units were built, creating pre-tax profits of some £606,000. Within four years, production of the 16-valve all-alloy Lotus engine had come on stream, although total car production had

The open-plan office accommodation at Hethel laid out by Chapman himself. The suggestion that Lotus should move to Norfolk was made by Tony Rudd.

dropped significantly to 2,822 units. Even so, the result of this change in manufacturing emphasis was a growth in pre-tax profits to £1,155,000.

Meanwhile, there were personnel changes, too. Out went Ron Hickman and, with John Frayling now acting as a free-lance consultant, in came the talented Oliver Winterbottom whose flair in the design studios would be a major factor in writing the next chapter in Lotus's history. Meanwhile, on the engineering side, Mike Kimberley − fresh from an impressive early career with Jaguar − was taken on board. Chapman also invited engine expert Tony Rudd to join the team from BRM, along with another gifted engineer, Ron Burr. As for the administration side, the post of Managing Director was given to Dennis Austin.

'One of the things I had to come to terms with when I joined Lotus was that everything was done in a tenth of the time it took at Jaguar' recalled Mike Kimberley. 'Time was money and both were short. This was crystallised by Chapman very early on in my days at Lotus. "There are fourteen days in every week: today, tonight, tomorrow and tomorrow night, etc.," he told me.'

IMPROVING THE IMAGE

Lotus had first begun to consider a replacement for the Lotus Ford tohc engine in 1966, just two years after the Elan had reached production. One factor which accelerated the need to develop a replacement for the old Ford-based unit was Ford's decision to drop the old 1,499cc engine in favour of a larger 1,599cc unit which boasted a new, deeper cylinder block and a crossflow-type cylinder head. However, special arrangements with Ford for supplies of the old blocks maintained the tohc unit in production − for the Europa − until 1975 (after all, Ford

themselves were to continue to use the Lotus tohc engine in the Cortina and later Escort until 1971). Nevertheless, the writing was on the wall and Chapman would have to look elsewhere.

Equally important, though, was Chapman's realisation that as long as he maintained his current line-up of cars, Lotus would always be perceived by a large percentage of the buying public as being a kit car manufacturer. This was simply because the Elan and Plus 2 had been available in customer-completion form from the early days − despite the fact that, proportionally, very few Plus 2s were sold in this form. If he was going to move his company up-market and give it a more exclusive image, Chapman needed a new model range.

The rigours of running a racing team and a sports car company are beginning to tell as this 1973 shot of Chapman clearly shows.

Production of the Lotus 2-litre engine went on stream in advance of the new car so a deal was agreed with Jensen over supplying the Lotus engine for the Jensen–Healey sports car.

Early examples of the stylish Lotus Elite undergoing pre-delivery inspection. Lotus developed a new vacuum-assisted resin-injection (VARI) system for moulding the bodies for this new range of cars.

Another important factor which Chapman had to consider was the forthcoming introduction of VAT which would spell the end of the tax exemption which had been enjoyed by cars completed by the customer. In addition, stringent safety and emission regulations in the States and special requirements for the EEC market (remember that Britain joined the Common Market in 1973) would have to be taken into account, not only by Lotus but by all motor manufacturers whose products

were being sold in these areas. Also, the market for the specialist sports car of the type Lotus were selling was changing. By the mid-1960s many manufacturers world-wide were offering similar cars to those being marketed by Lotus, while in the UK the popularity of the open-topped sports car was beginning to wane and there was a gradual but perceptible swing towards the closed coupe. Sports car passengers no longer found it fun to ride along with the top down and to be engulfed in smelly fumes from lorry exhausts. Chapman also harboured a dream: to drive Lotus into a position where they were less reliant on outside suppliers. The first step towards this was to design an engine which would be built totally in-house.

By 1967 the basic format of Lotus's new engine had been finalised. It would be a 2-litre unit made from aluminium with four valves per cylinder head. In fact, it was to be a family of engines based on a 4-litre V8 with a four-cylinder unit – effectively half the V8 – for use in the new range of sports road cars.

Stories of how Chapman, Ron Burr and Steve Sanville – on discovering that Vauxhall's new 2-litre sohc engine (on display at the 1967 Motor Show) was similar dimensionally to the Lotus unit – decided to use the Vauxhall cylinder block for testing purposes are now well documented. By 1971 all testing had been completed and Lotus unveiled their new engine which was to be manufactured in an impressive new plant, the investment in tooling alone reputedly costing some

£500,000. However, engine development was far in advance of the styling for Lotus's new range of cars so a deal was arranged with Jensen Motors Limited whereby Lotus would supply engines for the new Jensen–Healey sports car. (Engines supplied to Jensen were rated at 140bhp while engines later used in Lotus's own model range were rated at 160bhp.)

When production of the 'old' Elan finally ended in 1973 (the Europa remained on stream for another two years) Lotus had produced no fewer than 12,224 Elans and 5,200 Elan Plus 2s, the high spot being (as Albert Adams said) in 1969 when cars were coming off the line at the rate of 100 units per week. At the time of writing, Lotus have not since matched that figure.

A NEW LOTUS RANGE

The first of the new range of Lotus models came on stream, somewhat belatedly, in

The 2.2-litre Elite. Although small, the increase in engine size from the 2-litre version vastly improved the torque characteristics making the car much nicer to drive.

A rare photograph of Oliver
Winterbottom's styling proposal for
the Plus 2 replacement. The likeness
is clear. The design was not accepted
and Winterbottom developed the
wedge shape which became the Elite.

A scale model of the Elite undergoing
wind tunnel tests. Lotus's decision to
move their products up-market with a
new car and a new engine was a bold
step which only someone like
Chapman would contemplate.

1974. Known as the Elite (that name again!)
it was a wedge-shaped, two-door, four-seater
with a lift-up rear hatch. A year later came
the Eclat which was a notch back version of
the same car. This was followed in 1976 by
the Giugiaro-styled, mid-engined Esprit.
Four years later (spurred on by the need to
develop a larger 2.2-litre version of the Lotus
'four pot' for use in the Talbot Sunbeam
Lotus saloon) Lotus launched a new series of
the Elite, Eclat and Esprit. Fitted with a
2.2-litre engine (which was significantly
different from the units Lotus supplied to
Talbot) the increase in stroke size markedly
improved torque.

In the early days, Lotus's image and engine
quality did give rise for concern, as Fred
Bushell explained.

'Reliability-wise, it was a tragedy that
the people in America who were controlling
the US Jensen–Healey marketing (at this
time the Managing Director of Jensen
Motors Limited was Kjell Qvale, owner of a
sports car agency in San Francisco) were not
properly in contact with Jensen in West
Bromwich, who were manufacturing the
Jensen–Healey in the UK. The majority of
production went to the States and there was
no feedback on quality problems. During

this period we had the benefit of having Sir
Leonard Crossland as our Chief Executive.
He had retired from Ford and was brought in
because we were involved with our new car
programme. Had he known about the
Jensen–Healey problems he would have
done something about them.'

Despite Bushell's reassuring words, the
Jensen team did spend a considerable
amount of time with the Lotus development
engineers trying to cure oil surge, oil
aeration (at high revs) and loss of oil through
poor oil seals. Indeed, the pressure to sort out
these problems was such that it even affected
the launch date of the Jensen–Healey. However, since the Jensen–Healey was launched
in advance of Lotus's own model range, it did
allow a practical learning period during
which time problems with the 2-litre engine
could be rectified. Unfortunately, its early
reputation for poor reliability clearly did
neither firm any good.

Bushell was equally definite on the question
of whether the Elite did, indeed, elevate Lotus
in the way Chapman had envisaged.

'The problem with the Elite was that it
lacked the cachet of other £5,000 cars at the
time and customers still perceived us to be kit

*Early examples of the Lotus-powered
Jensen–Healey proved troublesome
and the car (and the engine) quickly
earned itself a bad reputation,
particularly in the States.*

car manufacturers', reflected Bushell during an interview in 1987. 'That was why, shortly afterwards, we looked at the viability of buying Aston Martin as a name to put on the front of our cars.' But, in Fred's opinion, the scheme was a non-starter. 'Although the spares operation and the property would have been of value, the AM product was costly to manufacture – and they would have wanted to retain their own vehicle in production.'

Clearly, the programme to introduce the Elite/Eclat range was a courageous one as it featured not only a whole new model range but a new engine as well. Few – if indeed any – other motor manufacturers would have undertaken such a step. 'The decision to go up-market,' said Mike Kimberley, 'put considerable strains on the company's team and a great deal of reorganisation had to be made, principally in design and development, as well as quality control.' But, no sooner had the new model range been frozen and the launch dates finalised, than the world was

set on course for an energy crisis which was to have far-reaching effects. In fact, at one stage it really looked as if Lotus would never recover. But, recover they did and by the mid-1970s the climate was a little more conducive for the sales of exclusive executive sports cars. By this time, the future of Jensen Motors Limited looked very bleak and Lotus were considering ways of boosting cash-flow by creating a high volume aspect to their business either through quantity supplies of their engines or by developing a new small sports car.

In the event, the latter course was taken. In 1976 Mike Kimberley and designer Oliver Winterbottom put together a programme for a small sports coupe which was presented to Chapman for his approval. Unfortunately, the timing of this proposal was wrong and Chapman, probably still smarting from the effects of the energy crisis and thinking of the investment that such a programme would need, rejected the idea. Just 655 Lotus cars had been built during 1975 and the future looked bleak indeed – exactly how bleak, only Chapman himself knew. And with money already committed to productionising the Eclat, there can have been precious little, if anything, left in the kitty to direct towards a programme such as this. (It was significant that 1976 was the year that Jensen Motors Limited finally went into receivership thereby marking the demise of the Jensen–Healey sports and GT which had been powered by the new Lotus 2-litre engine.)

A RISE IN FORTUNES . . .

As the trouble-strewn 1970s gave way to the more optimistic 1980s, however, conditions in the automotive world began to look brighter. To begin with, Lotus's own product range had now moved into high gear with the Elite, Eclat and Esprit models making a name for themselves in the exclusive – if

Chrysler's Des O'Dell approached Lotus over the supply of a 2.2-litre version of their 16-valve engine for fitting into his rally cars. The result was the Talbot Sunbeam Lotus.

An agreement was drawn up between Lotus and Talbot over the manufacture of the Sunbeam Lotus to homologation regulations. Here a consignment of cars leaves the Lotus works bound for Coventry.

With a 0–60mph (0–96.6kph) time of 6.7sec and a top speed of 125mph (201.2kph), the Sunbeam Lotus was the fastest hatchback of its day. It also won the World Rally Championship in 1981.

The interior of the Elite with its four seat accommodation.
Compare this to the interior of the Plus 2S in Chapter 3.

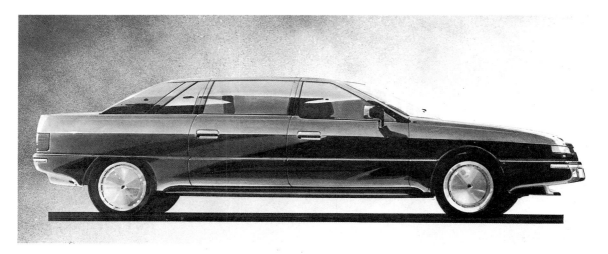

The styling proposal for the Lotus Eminence — the four-door
saloon Chapman hoped to build.

Another view of the Excel's interior. However, manufacture of the 1990s Elan meant that Lotus had to learn a whole new science in the art of mass production interior trimming methods.

unpredictable – high-performance sports car market. Production had increased to some 1,400 units (though even this represented only twenty-seven cars per week), while a recently signed deal with Chrysler paved the way for establishing another contract to supply Lotus engines to an outside manufacturer. Fred Bushell recalled the situation at the time:

'In 1976/77 we sat down and mapped out a corporate plan, indicating certain things we definitely wanted to do. One of those things was another 'tin fish', another car like the Lotus Cortina. We also said we wanted to take on external engineering.'

Des O'Dell needed an engine for his Chrysler Sunbeam rally cars as a way of making them into a competitive machine to see off the best that Ford and the Japanese could muster. The result was a car which was homologated as the Talbot Sunbeam Lotus (mid-way during negotiations in 1979 Chrysler sold out to Peugeot/Talbot) which won the World Rally Championship in 1981.

That year, Kimberley and Design Engineer Colin Spooner put forward the argument to Chapman that, in view of Lotus's more stable financial position, the company should begin looking at the feasibility of introducing a small, exclusive, quantity production sports car. In fact, the situation was not without a

Lotus's links with Toyota were to lead to them using a Toyota gearbox and final drive in the Excel which replaced the Elite and Eclat models.

degree of irony because Chapman was thinking more of a four-door saloon. (At the time, Chapman was driving a big Mercedes saloon and, since he had always built cars for his own requirements, most probably saw the need to begin producing something a little grander, something in the Jaguar image and in fact a styling proposal for the Lotus Eminence was produced.) Even so, Chapman agreed to their proposals with the proviso that an agreement could be reached with a major manufacturer for supplies of the fundamental mechanicals (suspension, drivetrain and so on), thereby keeping large-scale tooling investments to a minimum.

... A DROP
IN FORTUNES

However, Lotus's fortunes were suddenly swinging low once more − as Fred Bushell explained in 'Jabby' Crombac's excellent authorised biography on Chapman:

'"These were lean years," recalled Fred Bushell, "during which we plunged again. After American Express came in with their five-year loan, we had been able to advance despite the restrictions brought about by that particularly poor economic period, but by the autumn of 1982 we were operating at a very large trading loss. The figures for the period from August to December showed that we would have to pass the date when a repayment to American Express was due, causing us considerable embarrassment and putting us under "intensive care" by our bankers. Unfortunately, the situation was made worse because American Express were themselves undergoing a dramatic change, with new UK management being appointed who had no personal relationships with us and no real inside knowledge of the situation. American Express now viewed Lotus through eyes in New York, and relations became very strained simply because of a lack of appreciation of the problems. American Express were quite adamant that the loan repayment had to be made, so to give some temporary respite we arranged a private loan to reduce our indebtedness to them by a quarter-of-a-million pounds." '

In bald terms, this drop in fortunes looked like this on paper: production down from 1,200 units per year to some 383 − a significant drop − and pre-tax profits correspondingly dipping to just £461,000. (Compare this to the £1,283,000 at the

*Interior of the Excel showing just how far Lotus had come in
their design and trimming standards from the days of the Elan
in the mid-1960s.*

company's height.)

Contributing factors to this situation were the second oil crisis of the late 1970s, the poor relationship between Lotus and Rolls-Royce regarding sales of Lotus models in the States (in fact, sales there had almost ceased) and the loss of revenue from projects like the De Lorean and Sunbeam Lotus work. (Development on the De Lorean had finished and the future for Talbot's 'hot hatch' had already been foreshortened by the announcement of the closure of Linwood where the Sunbeam was manufactured.)

ENTER TOYOTA

Yet, even in such dire circumstances, Chapman's courage, confidence and boundless drive came to the fore and a plan was put in hand to improve the situation. This included a reduction in the prices of the Elite, Eclat and Esprit models and the start of a very fruitful relationship with the Japanese company Toyota. Once again, Bushell provides the background to this in Crombac's book:

' "When we were preparing a review of the business for 1980/81, although we believed that our decision to go up-market would eventually succeed, we came to the conclusion that we should not have abandoned entirely our traditional 'young executive' market, for which the Elan had been so suitable. Of course, it was lack of demand for cars in kit form, due to the taxation changes, which really made us decide to vacate it, but now we felt that it was still the major market into which the Lotus image fitted. We decided, therefore, that we should try to market a car at a price which the young, under-30 executive could afford." '

Clearly, the significance of Bushell's words here is that, despite Lotus's strong feelings that they ought to move their mainstream products into a more expensive sector of the specialist sports car market (encouraging buyers to perceive them to be no longer on a par with their old competitors, but edging into the TVR and Porsche bracket), inwardly they still thought of themselves as little different from ten years earlier.

Even so, Chapman made the initial overtures to Toyota (this was in advance of Toyota taking a stake in Lotus's operations) and negotiations were started, with Kimberley, Bushell and Chapman flying over to Japan to finalise the agreement. The deal was to be of mutual benefit: Toyota would supply Lotus with mechanical components for a revised Eclat model (known as the Excel, which utilised a Toyota-supplied gearbox and final drive), while Lotus agreed to undertake engineering development work on behalf of Toyota. Toyota were also to supply the parts necessary for the new, small sports car (the Elan's replacement) code-named the M90. Having established the deal with Toyota, the next hurdle was to arrange the finance with which to build the new car. Perhaps because of their newly-structured management profile, American Express were not interested in financing the programme. Neither were any of the other sources with whom Lotus held discussions. In reality, who would wish to become involved in putting up money for a new car when sales of the existing range were, to say the least, not in the best of health?

Bushell's observations on this period suggest that Chapman seemed not to be overworried by these circumstances; that, having established the route which would take M90 into production, if the whole house of cards (including Lotus Cars itself) fell to the ground, he at least had done his best.

DEATH OF A LEGEND

Many people, Bushell, Peter Kirwan-Taylor and the free-lance stylist John Frayling among them, have clear memories of Chapman during his last years. Bushell says he agrees strongly with observers that towards the end of the 1970s and the beginning of the 1980s Chapman took on more than he could cope with.

'People tended to treat Colin as an extrovert when, in fact, he was very much the opposite' explained Bushell during a recent interview with the author. 'Chapman was running a life's race. He sometimes came over as being brash but he didn't have time for niceties. He was an excellent time manager and wrote job list after job list.'

Frayling recalls that during this period, 'the old man' or 'ACBC' as he was so often referred to, often spent much of his time in his own office working on his next project – a microlight aircraft – and would sometimes need to be prised out to take phone calls or discuss day-to-day problems. His interest in Lotus Cars had greatly diminished. On a return flight from Paris, in particularly bad weather, the pilot of the aircraft in which Colin and Fred were flying said that they would have to land at Stansted. Colin appears to have become agitated at this and instructed the pilot to fly direct to Hethel, which he finally did, landing the plane in a severe cross-wind. Early the following morning, on 16 December 1982, Colin Chapman suffered a massive fatal heart attack.

Despite the growth of Lotus, by the early 1980s the company's image – something Lotus paid so much attention to – was still Chapman the man and his cars. Group Lotus *was* Chapman.

'I can't see a time when Mr Chapman will retire,' revealed Mike Kimberley to the author during a visit to the factory in November 1982. 'He has such an active brain that not to have something to occupy his mind would drive him mad. As he always says, "Old man Ferrari is thirty years older than me and still going strong, so I've got at least another thirty years left in the business."'

This remark was tragically transformed into stunning irony just weeks later, robbing the world of a man who had undoubtedly become a legend in his own lifetime.

In an interview just ten years earlier, which appeared in an October 1972 issue of *Autocar*, Ray Hutton intuitively commented:

'Anthony Colin Bruce Chapman is a dynamo. As Chairman of Lotus Group Car Companies Ltd., he runs on a very personal basis Britain's largest independent motor manufacturing business. He still lays out the basic designs for the cars they produce, and he still controls at first hand a Grand Prix racing team. Any one of these undertakings would keep an average man fully occupied. Chapman has successfully achieved all three activities for many years, working a constant seven-day week with no apparent signs of fatigue. As a personality he has the advantage of youth and a background of self-made success that allows him to communicate with people at all levels. He is sometimes charming, sometimes ruthless and sometimes disliked – but he is usually admired. In the past twenty years since he started producing specials in a stable in Hornsey, Chapman has become a tycoon. He has made a million – and Lotus have become a public company.'

To say that Chapman's death had a dramatic effect on the company and those with whom Lotus had financial connections is an understatement. However, despite his undisputed position within the company as Chairman and overall figurehead, it was not long before Fred Bushell was announced as replacement and plans were being made to ensure that Lotus's route to recovery was well mapped out. Orders for the Excel were exceeding even the company's highest hopes and the motor noters from Britain's automotive journals gave the car outstanding marks for performance and roadholding. Sleek, stylish, elegant and unquestionably quick, the new Excel, priced at £13,787, was a true 130mph (209.2kph) sports car. Not surprisingly, Lotus reckoned that by the end of 1983 they would have built some 800 cars – quite a recovery from the doldrums of a few years earlier when they produced 383 in a year. With the upsurge in sales, Lotus were able to pay off their debts to American Express and arrange new finance to underpin an elaborate expansion programme. This programme would incorporate the M90 sports car which had begun in 1981. Clearly, the future looked bright once more.

An artist's impression of the Lotus Esprit by Ital Design. From this a prototype was built, which formed the basis for the production mid-engined Esprit.

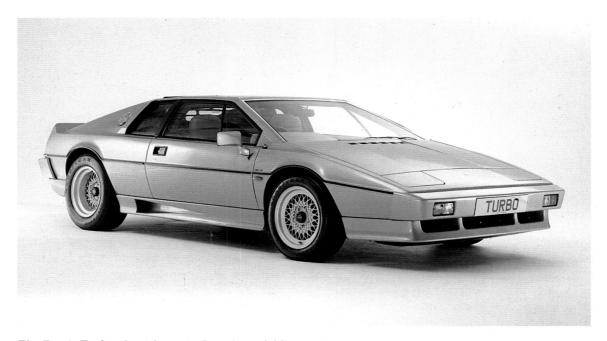

The Esprit Turbo, the only car in Lotus's model line-up to use a turbo version of their 2.2-litre 16-valve all-alloy engine. Its introduction pushed Lotus further up the exotic car manufacturer ladder.

The Lotus–Isuzu engine fitted to the latest Elan. Two versions are available: fuel injection and fuel injection with turbocharger.

The interior of the Elan showing the contemporary styled dashboard. Lotus were helped over its design and choice of instruments by GM in Detroit.

SON OF ELAN: M90?

While the 2.2-litre 16-valve engined cars would remain, Lotus were firmly committed to the introduction of an all-new sports car to replace the Elan. The basic layout for M90 was to be a front-engined, rear-wheel-drive sports car with a choice of either a 1.6- or 2-litre 16-valve twin ohc engine. In true Lotus tradition, M90 utilised a backbone chassis with a GRP body mounted onto it. Winterbottom's styling was thought to be pretty but hardly broke new ground, the flat sloping bonnet line influenced, perhaps, by the 'folded paper' shapes emanating from Italy.

Unfortunately, M90 went through a number of variations, none of which really caught anyone's imagination and the whole concept became stale even before it had reached production. (It seems that one problem the designers had to contend with in the early days was Chapman's continual intervention with new styling ideas he had seen on concept cars on exhibition around the world.) The trouble was that the front engine/rear-wheel-drive/backbone chassis package simply was not innovative in the way that the 1960s Elan had been. In truth, it lacked excitement and direction.

Following Chapman's tragic death the M90 project was frozen while the mainstream operations of Lotus could be restructured and it was not until November 1983 that the project was resurrected. To discover whether the proposed M90 design really did have a future a prototype was built and put on the road in March 1984. Among its features were small jump seats in the rear, a split hood design which allowed the overhead section to be removed leaving the rear in position if desired, and pop-up headlights set into the front corners of the wings. At this point, M90's fate was sealed and later that year the decision was taken to terminate the programme in its current form. While Mike Kimberley and the rest of the team were

adamant that a new, volume sports car was badly needed to swell the Lotus product line, M90 was not the car to do it. It was too like a TVR and simply was not 'Lotus' enough.

Meanwhile, Lotus's fortunes had been enhanced by the negotiations which had been taking place behind the scenes with both Toyota and David Wickens of British Car Auctions and which were approved in August 1983. The resulting financial restructuring of Lotus was to have a marked effect on the decision to include a new small sports car in the Lotus line-up.

SON OF ELAN: X100?

In January 1985 the M90's successor – the X100 – was commissioned. However, it was to have a fundamental difference to its predecessor: it was to be front-wheel-drive. By the mid-1980s so many of the world's manufacturers were developing and producing FWD products that, clearly, a car with a conventional drivetrain layout would appear 'old hat' to the buying public. Indeed, the average driver seemed to prefer front-wheel-drive. Another key factor in this decision was that by this time Roger Becker and his team in engineering development (in line with Lotus's policy to take on engineering work for other manufacturers world-wide) had been involved with around fourteen or so FWD programmes. One in particular, for an American company, had changed a car from something of a handful into one which had very good handling, due entirely to Lotus development. Moreover, since X100 would utilise a Toyota power pack, the unit identified for the job was to be the 1.6-litre, 16-valve, 120bhp Corolla engine.

Body-wise, the X100's designer was Peter Stevens. His brief was to create a coupe and a soft-top, both of which had clear similarities to the 'Etna' supercar project which had been styled by Giugiaro. This was the car which would be powered by Lotus's B8 engine and was displayed at the 1984 London Show where it attracted considerable attention. Somewhat surprisingly, since the soft-top was to be the more important of the two cars, the first X100 to be styled was the coupe. It seems that the reason for this was that the team felt that the coupe version would be the easier to create – despite the fact that most stylists agree that the optimum solution for a rag top is *not* by way of a fixed-head variant. Moreover, Stevens was never happy designing a car whose lines were clearly linked to another model. Worse, the Lotus board were never entirely happy with the Etna model and decided to cancel the programme. This simply left the X100, although its future was also in question. Much cutting, cleaning and carving was done in an effort to rescue X100 so that, despite everyone's doubts, it could be

made attractive. Towards the end of 1985, work on X100 slowed as enthusiasm waned and Spooner, Stevens and the team began putting their heads together. Kimberley described the X100 coupe as looking like a 'pregnant guppy' and was clearly worried that, despite its FWD layout, its shape was neither fresh nor fascinating.

Meanwhile, Kimberley became embroiled in negotiations which would result in General Motors acquiring a controlling interest in the Hethel-based company and spent a considerable time touring the Lotus dealers in an effort to instil confidence in the products and explain that, despite the new-found links with Detroit, Lotus would continue to make its own decisions. The agreement between Lotus and GM was finalised in February 1986 and the following month

The new and the old. An Elan S4 drophead and a pre-production model of the latest Elan outside Lotus's Hethel-based headquarters.

Mike Kimberley has said that Lotus could have simply taken the old Elan and revamped it. But it is not Lotus's way of doing things and they look towards the 1990s with confidence, knowing the latest Elan will be a winner.

A rear three-quarter shot showing the neat alloy road wheels and the boot-mounted spoiler. A considerable amount of time was spent in the wind tunnel to perfect the car's performance in side winds.

*The new Lotus being unveiled at the 1989 London Motor Show.
From his first talks with Colin Chapman, Mike Kimberley had
waited some fifteen years for this moment to give the world a
new Lotus Elan.*

Kimberley, with characteristic Chapman-like charisma, cancelled the X100 because it was not seen to be the volume sports car to carry Lotus into the 1990s. What was needed, he felt, was a 'clean sheet of paper' approach to the project.

SON OF ELAN: M100!

At a memorable meeting held in March that year, Kimberley drew together not only members of Lotus's own design department but also Ital Design and GM's designers headed by Chuck Jordan. As a hands-on manager, Kimberley first and foremost had to fire his teams with enthusiasm so that they would give of their best. Rightly or wrongly, by creating this competitive situation he achieved his goal. Certainly, he had to ensure that, with two failures behind them, the third styling proposal was right. M100 – as the project had now become – had to be stunning and dramatic. Top on their list of priorities for a power unit for the new car was that, ideally, the engine should be at the drawing-board stage so that Lotus could have their own design input. As Ian Adcock, Lotus's Public Relations Manager, explained:

'There were a number of factors involved in the choice of engine for the new M100. We needed a front-wheel-drive unit and by the time the definitive M100 programme was given the green light by the Lotus board we realised that Toyota would not wish to divulge information to us on the design of any new engine they may have had on their drawing board. GM already had an interest in Isuzu, who we knew to be developing a very neat compact engine which we felt would be ideal for the M100.'

In fact, Lotus's engineers contributed over a redesign of the Isuzu engine's induction system and its electronic engine management system. By February 1987, a ten-year agreement had been drawn up with Isuzu for the supply of the still-to-be-productionised power unit while the launch date of the new car was to be the autumn of 1989.

Meanwhile, work on the styling proposal for the M100 was moving ahead at an exciting pace with Spooner, Stevens and the team managing to create just the right shape. The Lotus board chose this in favour of the designs from Ital Design and GM, although it seems that these two proposals did contribute to the fine tuning of the British design. (The M100 was to be a soft-top only – no consideration being given to a coupe version.) From this point on, the whole M100 team were more dedicated to the design of the new Lotus sports car than ever they had been with the previous programmes. Spooner said that they had been trying to grasp the flavour of the original Elan's philosophy and had not succeeded – their sense of direction with M90 and X100 had been very vague. Now, however, the mists had cleared and enthusiasm was running high.

The man responsible for the car's interior design and the sourcing of parts (such as instruments, controls and so on – the myriad of bits and pieces inside a modern car) was Simon Cox. Starting with a collection of parts it was then down to him to arrange them together to form the impressive and stylish dashboard. It was here that GM helped considerably, although the trick was to ensure that having grouped the units together the finished design looked complete and integrated rather than just a selection of *ad hoc* controls and dials. On the styling side, Stevens was adding the final touches to the shape which would form M100. The very compact design of the Isuzu power unit allowed for a very short engine compartment. Moreover, to keep the line of the car neat and uncluttered when the hood was down Stevens decided that it should be folded behind a hinged panel, rather like that used on Rootes's Sunbeam Alpine and Tiger sports cars of the 1960s.

When all was complete in November 1986, a one-fifth scale model was taken to the Imperial College of Science and Technology in London, where it was tested in a wind tunnel. Clearly, aerodynamics would be a crucial factor in the behaviour of the new Lotus and the model's performance did not disappoint its creators: with the hood up it registered a coefficient of drag (Cd) of 0.32 and a lift coefficient of −0.17. Tests were also done to assess the car's reaction to side winds and slight alterations were made to the design of the front spoiler and the height of the windscreen and boot lid. Finally, attention was turned to ensuring that interior buffeting was reduced to a minimum and to this end the curvature of the 'A' posts was changed.

Production engineering was another area where the Lotus engineers expended considerable effort. The problems which faced Hickman and his team in the 1960s were emerging again twenty-five or so years later on the new Elan programme: to design a build system which would make the car as cheaply and effectively and to the highest quality possible time and time again. The assembly period for the Esprit was rated at 550 hours and Lotus had calculated a self-imposed time limit of 178 hours for the new Elan. This would mean that the actual assembly process would need to be as efficient and cost effective as possible. Lotus would have to commit themselves to tooling processes in advance so that production could take advantage of volume manufacturing techniques.

The power train for the new Elan would be available in two engine types, both based on a 1,588cc 16-valve unit with Delco electronic engine control and Rochester fuel injection systems. With this specification the power output was rated at 138bhp at 7,200rpm, the turbocharged version producing a very healthy 165bhp at 6,600rpm.

'We believed Lotus had the expertise and technology to develop an exceptional handling front-wheel-drive sports car with a high degree of manoeuvrability and stability that would set new world standards and provide outstanding grip in all weather conditions' said Mike Kimberley. 'We believe that a contemporary sports car of under 2 litres should instil great confidence for the average driver while rewarding the more skilful with great handling. Front-wheel-drive also gives a 135mph (217.3kph) sports car like the Elan a high degree of stability and manoeuvrability.'

Rigidity was a key factor in designing the chassis, floorpan and body attachments. The chassis frame itself is an octagonal section backbone frame which runs back from the scuttle picking up with the rear suspension mounting points. In an effort to simplify assembly and servicing, a front subframe was designed which carried the power train and the front suspension attaching to the main chassis at its front face below the bulkhead. The floorpan is manufactured from polyester resin and to increase stiffness still further, it is strengthened by the addition of reinforced steel outriggers which are let into the 'A' and 'B' posts, the toe board, the rear cross brace and the sills, the outriggers being riveted and bonded to the floorpan. The outriggers also form the locating points for the door hinges, the seat belt anchorages and the seat runners. Like the earlier Elan, the body/chassis structure is such that the bodywork itself is a non-stressed unit.

Hand-in-glove with the desire to create outstanding handling through a rigid body/chassis unit, the Lotus engineers developed a revolutionary front suspension design. The basis of this design is an aluminium alloy mounting frame known as a raft − one on the nearside front and a second on the offside front of the car. In turn, each raft is located on

(Overleaf) *The car on its special turntable on the Lotus stand at the Earls Court Show in October 1989.*

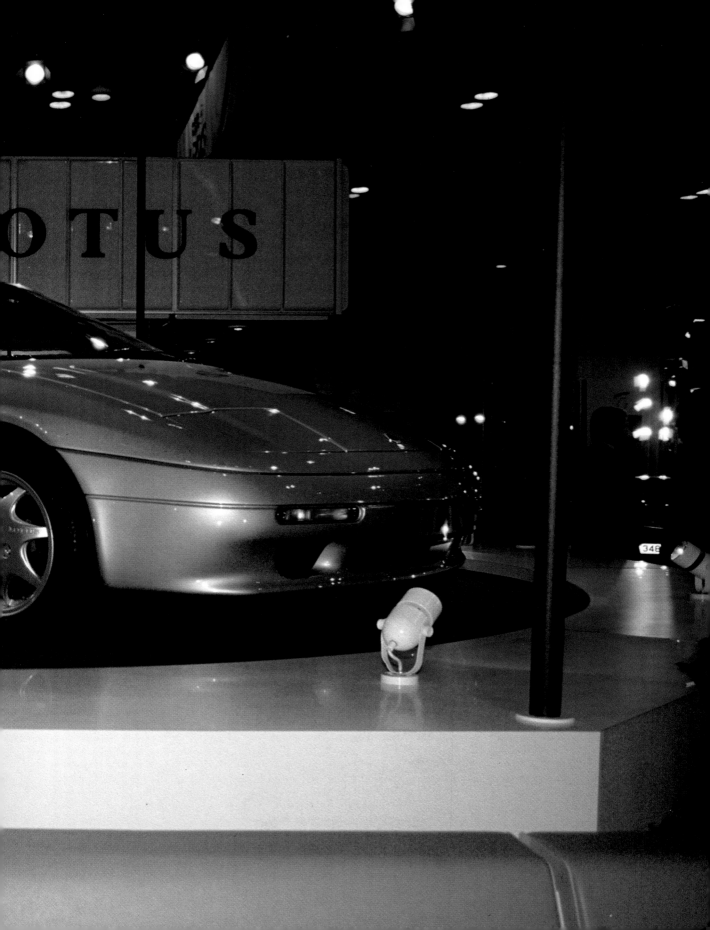

1989 LOTUS ELAN – TECHNICAL SPECIFICATION

ENGINE
Configuration: 16 valves, dohc four-cylinder 'Isuzu-Lotus'
Capacity: (cc/cu in) 1,588/246
Power: 130bhp/97 kW @ 7,200 rpm
Torque: 105 lb ft/142 Nm @ 4,200 rpm
Bore (mm/in): 80/3.15
Stroke (mm/in): 79/3.11
Compression ratio: 10.0:1
Valve actuation: Belt driven double overhead camshafts with direct
  acting hydraulic tappets
Fuelling: Electronic multi-point fuel injection
Construction: Cast iron block, aluminium alloy cylinder head
Ignition: Electronic distributor ignition
Alternator: 60-amp
Oil cooler: 24-row

TRANSMISSION
Type: Five-speed manual gearbox
Ratios: (mph/km per 1,000 rpm)
First: 3.333:1 (4.84/7.78)
Second: 1.916:1 (8.41/13.53)
Third: 1.333:1 (12.09/19.46)
Fourth: 1.027:1 (15.70/25.25)
Fifth: 0.829:1 (19.45/31.29)
Reverse: 3.583:1
Final drive ratio: 4.117:1
Clutch: Single plate dry disc diaphragm clutch 8.46in/215mm

BODY AND CHASSIS
Body: Multi-piece bonded, riveted and bolted GRP and steel
  composite structure. Single piece VARI floorpan moulding.
  Welded steel sill/outrigger assemblies.
Chassis: Steel fabrication with corrosion protection by zinc coating,
  chip resistant polyurethane coating and wax injection into closed
  box sections.
  Backbone chassis extends rearwards from front bulkhead, and
  incorporates rear suspension pick-up points, bolting rigidly to
  body shell structure.
  Front longeron/underframe assembly bolts onto front of backbone
  frame, incorporating front suspension pick-up points, engine
  mountings and front energy absorbing structure. Complete
  subframe assembly, including powertrain, is detachable.
Front suspension: Independent by unequal length wishbones.
  Coaxial coil springs and dampers. Tubular anti-roll bar via drop
  links from chassis. Longitudinal compliance by individual
  aluminium alloy subframes.

PERFORMANCE
Maximum speed: 122
  mph/196 kph
0–60 mph: 7.6s
0–100 kph: 8.2s
Standing ¼ mile/
  400m 16.1s

FUEL CONSUMPTION

	mpg	l/100km
Urban	25.9	10.9
Steady 56 mph (90 kph)	40.8	6.9
Steady 75 mph (120 kph)	35.2	8.0

STANDARD EQUIPMENT
Power assisted steering – optional
Tilt-adjustable steering column
Leather rim steering wheel
Alloy wheels
Central door locking
Electric windows

Electric door mirrors
Electrically heated door mirrors

Leather and cloth upholstery
Metallic paint – optional
Bronze tinted glass
Remote fuel filler release
Radio/cassette player –
  standard
Premium radio/cassette
  player with RDS optional
Laminated windscreen

Rear suspension: Independent by upper link and wide-based lower
  wishbone.
  Coaxial coil springs and dampers. Solid anti-roll bar via drop links
  from chassis.,
Steering: Rack-and-pinion
  Turns, lock-to-lock: 3.1
  Turning circle (between kerbs): (ft/m) 35/10.66
Wheels: Lotus design 6.5J × 15 Cast aluminium alloy
Tyres: Michelin MXV2 205/50 VR 15
Spare tyre: Space-saver T105/70R14
Brakes: Type and size: Front: Ventilated discs with single cylinder
  floating callipers (10in/256mm dia); Rear: Solid discs with single
  cylinder floating callipers and integral mechanical parking brake
  (7.3in/236 mm dia)
Actuation: Tandem master cylinder with diagonal split circuit
  In-line rear brake pressure compensating valve for each circuit

ELAN S/E (Variations)

ENGINE
Power: 165 bhp/123 kW@6,600 rpm
Torque: 148 lb ft/200 Nm@4,200 rpm
Compression ratio: 8.2:1
Ignition: Distributorless ignition, controlled by ECM
Turbocharger: Water-cooled turbocharger with air-to-air
  intercooler
Boost pressure: 9.4 psi/0.6 bar

TRANSMISSION
Ratios: (mph/km per 1,000 rpm)
First: 3.333:1 (5.20/8.35)
Second: 1.916:1 (9.04/14.54)
Third: 1.333:1 (12.99/20.90)
Fourth: 1.027:1 (16.86/27.18)
Fifth: 0.829:1 (20.89/33.61)
Final drive ratio: 3.833:1
Clutch: Single plate dry disc diaphragm clutch 8.86in/225mm

BODY AND CHASSIS
Steering: Rack-and-pinion with hydraulic power assistance
  Turns, lock-to-lock: 2.9
Tyres: Michelin MXX2 205/50 ZR15

DIMENSIONS
Kerb weight (lbs/kg): 2,249/1,020

PERFORMANCE
Maximum speed: 137 mph/220kph
  0–60 mph 6.7s
  0–100kph 7.2s
  Standing ¼ mile/400m 15.4s

FUEL CONSUMPTION

	mpg	l/100km
Urban:	26.2	10.8
Steady 56 mph (90 kph)	42.2	6.7
Steady 75 mph (120 kph)	31.8	8.9

INSTRUMENTATION
Digital clock

DIMENSIONS (in/mm)
Wheelbase: 88.6/2,250
Front track: 58.5/1,486
Rear track: 58.5/1,486
Overall length: 149.7/3,803
Overall width
(excl. mirrors): 68.3/1,734
(incl. mirrors): 74.3/1,885
Overall height (soft-top
  raised): 48.4/1,230
Ground clearance: 5.1/130

Fuel tank capacity
(gal/l): 10.2/46.4
Fuel grade: 95 RON unleaded/
  97 RON leaded
Kerb weight
(lbs/kg): 2,198/997
Weight distribution
(% front/rear): 66/34
Cd (hood up): 0.34
Cd (hood down): 0.38

to the chassis frame. In a conventional wishbone suspension the rubber bushes used in the locating points are – by necessity – of soft rubber to help reduce road noise and vibration. The penalty, however, is suspension geometry changes as the car moves. The benefit of introducing the raft as an intermediary locating point is that it introduces the opportunity for the designers to create longitudinal suspension compliance – which is only marginally detrimental to handling and nothing like that of a conventional wishbone arrangement – while the vertical and lateral suspension movements are reduced dramatically, thereby improving handling and stability. This is achieved by using stiff rubber/metal bushes on the raft/chassis mountings which control vertical and lateral movement while the mounting which gives longitudinal movement is a much softer rubber-only unit.

Also, this system ensures that the car's roll centre remains more constant and resists body roll better so that softer road springs can be used. In addition, since there is so little change in castor action, a lower castor angle can be specified which means that lower steering forces are required. At the rear, the suspension layout is based on that of the Excel, modified for mass production and comprises an independent set-up with an upper link and a wide-based lower wishbone. The steering is provided by an Ad West rack with a turns ratio of 3.1:1 on the base model and 2.9:1 on the power-assisted rack fitted to the Elan Turbo.

When it came to body manufacture, despite carrying out in-depth research into current processes and materials, Lotus concluded that their own vacuum-assisted resin-injected (VARI) process was still the best available for moulding body forms, although the opportunity was taken to employ a larger number of sub-assembly body moulds than was currently being used on the Excel and Esprit in order to allow for greater freedom of design later on. Moreover, Lotus patented a system called 'Fibreform' which allows self-locating preformed fibre reinforcement to be used in conjunction with the VARI moulding process. In addition, the wearing surfaces of the body moulding tools were given an electroplated nickel lining to vastly improve their service life and ensure a very high degree of body panel finish so that very little preparation is needed before starting the painting process. Also, because there is virtually no shrinkage during curing this gives a high degree of control over body panel dimensions.

BUILDING FOR THE FUTURE

With the new Elan, Lotus intend to return to their manufacturing levels of the late 1960s and have invested some £35 million at Hethel to engineer and manufacture their cars. Lotus are determined to continue in Chapman's footsteps in making the company more and more autonomous. With these new manufacturing processes and the lessons learned in developing the new car, the Elan will clearly stand the company in good stead for the future. It is very much a flagship for Lotus's engineering capabilities. As for the long term, Mike Kimberley said that the Elan,

'. . . means that Lotus will continue to establish itself as one of the most pre-eminent high-performance car manufacturers in the world. It would have been the easiest thing in the world for us to have copied the old Elan and just put a different body-style on it and make it look a bit more modern. But that isn't what Lotus is about. Lotus is all about setting new vehicle dynamic standards for the world and creating a unique sports car, an image builder and I believe we have done that.'

Lotus Clubs and Services

BRITISH-BASED CLUBS

Club Elite
(Elite register, makes Elite parts, knows
  sources of spares)
Nick Raven
Little Guesting
15 Teatling Road
Countesthorpe
Leicestershire LE8 3RD
Tel: 0533 773630

Club Lotus
Margaret Arnold
Club Lotus
PO Box 8
Dereham
Norfolk
Tel: 0362 694459

East Anglia Lotus Club
Mark Rolph
Holme Lea
Low Common
Ashby St Mary
Norwich
Norfolk NR14 7BQ
Tel: 0508 43758

Historic Lotus Register
(Lotus Mark I–XVII, 1953–1960)

Victor Thomas (*Lotus XI Registrar*)
Historic Lotus Register
Badgers Farm
Short Green
Winfarthing
Norfolk IP22 2EE
Tel: 0953 860508

Graham Capel (*Newsletter Editor and Mark
  VIII/X Registrar*)
Nye's Place
Rusper Road
Newdigate
Surrey RH5 5BX
Tel: 0293 84541

Mike Marsden (*Secretary, Historic Lotus
  Register* and *Mark XI Registrar*)
Orchard House
Wotton Road
Rangeworthy
Bristol
Avon BS17 5NA
Tel: 0454 22266

Historic Sports Car Club
Brian Cocks
Chief Executive
West Lodge
Norton
Wiltshire SN16 0JS

Historic Sports Car Club (Lotus Section)
George Rance (*Elite Type Fourteen owner*)
36 Mayfield Avenue
Grove
Wantage
Oxfordshire OX12 7ND

Lotus Cortina Register
David Missions
Fern Leigh
Hornash Lane
Shadowhurst
Ashford
Kent TN26 1HT
Tel: 0233 733406

PR
Duncan Tough
Nethermore Farm
Naish Hill
Lacock
West Chippenham
Wiltshire SN15 2QH
Tel: 0249 73294

Lotus Drivers Club
Laurie Barton
15 Pleasant Way
Leamington Spa
Warwickshire CV32 5XA

47 Club
Pat Thomas
Kelvedon Motors
Bourne Road
Spalding
Lincolnshire
Tel: 0775 5457/68097

Lotus Seven Club
David Mirylees (*Secretary*)
18 St James
Beaminster
Dorset DT8 3PW
Tel: 0308 863164

R P Wood (*Northern Owners*)
30 Queensway
Newton
Chester
Cheshire CH2 1PG
Tel: 0244 45327

Dick Dixon (*Hertfordshire Area*)
90 Cappell Lane
Stanstead Abbotts
Ware
Hertfordshire SG12 8BY

Peter Burgess (*Press Officer*)
56 Meadow Walk
Harpenden
Hertfordshire AL5 5TG
Tel: 05827 61625

OVERSEAS CLUBS

Australia

Club Lotus Australia (National HQ)
PO Box 220
Strathfield
New South Wales 2135
Australia

(There are branches in Victoria,
Queensland and South Australia)

Belgium

Club Lotus Belgie
Jette-Fooz
276 Route de Wasseiges
B–5022 Cognelee
Belgium

Canada

Lotus Car Club of British Columbia
PO Box 46467
Station G
Vancouver
British Columbia V6R 4G7
Canada

Canadian Lotus Club
340 Dixon Road
Western Ontario M9R 1T1
Canada

Denmark

Lotus Club of Denmark
Erling Glerup (LCD)
Toftevaenget 2
4200 Slagelse
Denmark

France

Club Lotus France
Alain Celerier
Club Lotus France
La Pelouse 72160
Tuffe
France

Germany

Lotus Seven Club Deutschland
Richard Spelberg
Postfach 111014
4000 Düsseldorf 11
West Germany
Tel: (Home) 0211 681766

Can also provide sales literature, workshop manuals and parts lists for marks and types ranging from the Mark 6 onwards. The address to write to for this is:

Richard Spelberg
Bodinusstrasse 9
D4000 Düsseldorf 1
West Germany

Lotus Freunde Deutschland
H G Stellwagen
Birkenweg 1
D–6501 Heidesheim
West Germany

Holland

Lotus Seven Club Nederland
Wolbrantskerkweg 4
1069 CX Amsterdam
Holland

Japan

Lotus Club Japan
Mr Paul Ishiyama
14–3, 2–Chome
Higashi
Shibuya-ku
Tokyo
Japan

Luxembourg

Lotus 7 Club Luxembourg
21 Rue Sangen
L-5866 Hesperange
Luxembourg

New Zealand

Club Lotus New Zealand
PO Box 27016
Mt Roskill
Auckland
New Zealand

South Africa

The Lotus Register
(Originally called the Historic Lotus Register, renamed 1985)
Des Cain (*Chairman*)
PO Box 6513
Brackendowns
1454 South Africa

Sweden

Lotus Car Club of Sweden
Dane Glantz
Langgatan 49
561 34 Huskvarna
Sweden

Lotus Seven Club Sweden
S Appolloyagen 36B
552 48 Jonkoping
Sweden

Switzerland

Lotus Schweiz
Unterwertstrasse 5
CH−8152
Glattbrugg
Switzerland

Fredy Kumschick
CH−6247 Schotz
Luzernerstrasse
Switzerland
Tel: 045 713771
Fax: 045 713774

Swiss Lotus Team
Luca Pedotti
Querstrasse 4
CH−8424 Embrach
Switzerland
Tel: 018 654492

Lotus Seven Owners Switzerland
Roger Savare
Postfach 57
CH−6000
Luzern 15
Switzerland
Tel: 041 222658

United States of America

Lotus Corps
76 N Peck
La Grange
Illinois 60525
USA

League of Lotus Owners
8660 S E King Road
Portland
Oregon 97266
USA

Lotus Cortina of America Register
253 Diablo Avenue
Mountain View
California 94043
USA

Lotus Ltd (Lotus Remarque)
PO Box L
College Park
Maryland 20740
USA

Lotus West Car Club
Steve Griffin
217 19th Street
Manhattan Beach
California 90266
USA
Tel: (Hotline): 213 4921556

Club Elite
Michael Ostrov
6238 Ralston Avenue
Richmond
California 94805
USA
Tel: (Home): 415 2327764
Tel: (Work): 415 4654040

The Great Lakes Lotus Club
19511 Lowell
Detroit
Michigan 48203
USA

Lotus Formula Ford Register
c/o Vern Jaques
1129 Monserate Avenue
Chula Vista
California 92011
USA
Tel: 619 4201958

New England Lotus Lovers
11 Popular Street
Ipswich
Massachusetts 01938
USA

Golden Gate Lotus Club
David Anderson
PO Box 117303
Burlingame
California 94011
USA

Lotus Twenty-Three Users Group
11 Rocky Ridge Lane
Farmington
Connecticut 06032
USA

Evergreen Lotus
11232 312th NE
Carnation
Washington 98014
USA

USEFUL COMPANIES FOR THE ELAN OWNER

AKS Engineering
Church Street
Trawden
Nr Colne
Lancashire
Tel: 0282 867087

Automobile Workshops
Lancaster Mews
Richmond Hill
Richmond
Surrey
Tel: 081 940 9252

Bell and Colvill
Epsom Road
West Horsley
Surrey
Tel: 0486 54671

Burton Performance Centre
621/631 Eastern Avenue
Barkingside
Ilford
Essex
Tel: 081 554 2281

Ceandess
Dixon Street
Wolverhampton
West Midlands
Tel: 0902 51195

Christopher Neil Sportscars
Middlewich Road
Northwich
Cheshire
Tel: 0606 47914

C J Foulds (Motors)
Commercial Mills
Frith Street
Huddersfield
West Yorkshire
Tel: 0484 34743

Classicar Automotive
St Michaels Way
Middlewich
Cheshire
Tel: 0606 846474

Dave Gallop AutoCare
Unit 1
Ironmould Lane
Brislington
Bristol
Avon
Tel: 0272 714968

Ed Winter Engineering Developments
9 Witham Close
Bedford
Bedfordshire
Tel: 0234 68803

Evante Cars
Cradge Bank
Spalding
Lincolnshire
Tel: 0775 4846

Fibreglass Services
Charlton Saw Mills
Charlton
Singleton
Chichester
West Sussex
Tel: 0243 63320

Kelvedon Motors
Bourne Road
Spalding
Lincolnshire
Tel: 0775 5457

Ken Myers Partnership
c/o Harbour Road Service Station
Northampton
Northamptonshire
Tel: 0604 843019

Len Street
Drayton Gardens
London SW10
Tel: 071 373 7200

The London Lotus Centre
Ballards Yard
High Street
Edgware
Middlesex
Tel: 081 952 5578

Lothian Sportscars
11 East Milton Road
Edinburgh
Scotland
Tel: 0316 698444

Malmesbury Specialist Cars
Crudwell Road
Malmesbury
Wiltshire
Tel: 0666 22309

Mike Spence
School Green
Shinfield
Reading
Berkshire
Tel: 0734 883140

Norfolk Motor Company
242 Spronson Road
Norwich
Norfolk
Tel: 0603 416613

Paul Matty Sportscars
12 Old Birmingham Road
Lickey End
Bromsgrove
Worcestershire
Tel: 0527 35656

Performance Unlimited
290 Wesborough Road
Westcliff-on-Sea
Essex
Tel: 0702 40954

Quorn Engine Developments
Soar Road
Quorn
Nr Loughborough
Leicestershire
Tel: 0509 412317

Speedex Autoparts
Westbury
Wiltshire
Tel: 0373 826334

Spydersport
Station Road Industrial Estate
Whittlesey
Peterborough
Cambridgeshire
Tel: 0733 205639

Terry Carthy Sportscars
4E Pepper Road
Bramhall Moor Industrial Park
Hazel Grove
Manchester
Tel: 061 456 5341

Twin Cam Techniques
Brindley Road
Dodwells Bridge Industrial Estate
Hinckley
Leicestershire
Tel: 0455 619006

Vulcan Engineering
185 Uxbridge Road
London W7
Tel: 081 579 3202

Yardley Wood Service Station
1016 Yardley Wood Road
Yardley Wood
Birmingham
West Midlands
Tel: 021 474 4972

Bibliography

Crombac, Gerard *Colin Chapman. The Man and His Cars* (Patrick Stephens, 1986).

Harvey, Chris *Lotus. A Competition Survey of the Sports, GT and Touring Cars* (Osprey, 1980).

Harvey, Chris *Lotus: The Elite, Elan, Europa* (The Oxford Illustrated Press, 1982).

Pritchard, Anthony *Lotus. The Sports Racing Cars* (Patric Stephens, 1987).

Robinshaw, Paul and Ross, Christopher *The Original 1962–1973 Lotus Elan* (MRP, 1989).

Robson, Graham *The Third Generation Lotuses* (MRP, 1983).

Smith, Ian H. *The Story of Lotus* (MRP, 1978).

Wilkins, Miles *Lotus Twin-Cam Engine* (Osprey, 1988).

Index